T0207127

Productizing Quantum Computing

Bring Quantum Computing Into Your Organization

Dhairyya Agarwal
Shalini D
Srinjoy Ganguly

Apress®

Productizing Quantum Computing: Bring Quantum Computing Into Your Organization

Dhairyya Agarwal
California, USA

Shalini D
Tirupur, India

Srinjoy Ganguly
Ghaziabad, India

ISBN-13 (pbk): 978-1-4842-9984-5
https://doi.org/10.1007/978-1-4842-9985-2

ISBN-13 (electronic): 978-1-4842-9985-2

Managing Director, Apress Media LLC: Welmoed Spahr
Acquisitions Editor: Smriti Srivastava
Development Editor: Laura Berendson
Editorial Assistant: Shaul Elson

Cover designed by eStudioCalamar

Cover image designed by Freepik (www.freepik.com)

Distributed to the book trade worldwide by Springer Science+Business Media New York, 1 New York Plaza, Suite 4600, New York, NY 10004-1562, USA. Phone 1-800-SPRINGER, fax (201) 348-4505, e-mail orders-ny@ springer-sbm.com, or visit www.springeronline.com. Apress Media, LLC is a California LLC and the sole member (owner) is Springer Science + Business Media Finance Inc (SSBM Finance Inc). SSBM Finance Inc is a **Delaware** corporation.

For information on translations, please e-mail booktranslations@springernature.com; for reprint, paperback, or audio rights, please e-mail bookpermissions@springernature.com.

Apress titles may be purchased in bulk for academic, corporate, or promotional use. eBook versions and licenses are also available for most titles. For more information, reference our Print and eBook Bulk Sales web page at http://www.apress.com/bulk-sales.

Any source code or other supplementary material referenced by the author in this book is available to readers on GitHub. For more detailed information, please visit https://www.apress.com/gp/services/source-code.

Paper in this product is recyclable

Table of Contents

About the Authors

Dhairyya Agarwal is a product manager at Microsoft solving problems in the email and collaboration security space. He received his master's degree from Carnegie Mellon University in software management. Dhairyya has delivered on many initiatives focused on improving retention, activation, and engagement. He has also worked on many zero-to-one products to enable businesses to enter new markets. He is based in Mountain View, California.

Shalini D is a quantum AI researcher at Fractal QuantumAI Lab researching quantum algorithms at the intersection of quantum chemistry and quantum machine learning. Previously, she was a systems engineer at Infosys, working as a core customization API developer. Shalini completed her master's in quantum technologies at CSIC (Spanish National Research Council) at the Universidad Internacional Menendez Pelayo in Spain. Her research includes semiconductor spin qubits, quantum machine learning, and quantum chemistry. She has taught quantum computing (basic to advanced) at many universities, including the Vellore Institute of Technology in India. She has also delivered several lectures at various universities. Her Udemy course on the Qiskit developer exam is highly rated and a global bestseller.

Srinjoy Ganguly is a quantum AI research scientist at Fractal QuantumAI Lab and a clinical professor of the "Practice for Quantum Technology" course at Woxsen University. He is also an associate supervisor at the University of Southern Queensland in Australia, supervising PhD students in quantum machine learning. He is an IBM Qiskit advocate and an IBM quantum educator with more than five years of experience in quantum technologies. Srinjoy is the author of the book *Quantum Computing with Silq Programming* and has published several research papers on quantum chemistry, quantum machine learning, and quantum NLP. Additionally, he has published articles in Nature India, the Quantum Insider, and DZone. He possesses a triple master's in quantum technologies, quantum computing technology, and artificial intelligence (AI) from CSIC-UIMP in Spain, Universidad Politecnica de Madrid, and the University of Southampton, respectively. Furthermore, he has two Udemy courses with 15,000+ students enrolled globally, contributes to podcasts, and delivers lectures on quantum technologies. His research interests include superconducting quantum circuits, hybrid superconducting-semiconducting heterostructures (1D and 2D), topological quantum computing, spin qubits, quantum machine learning, quantum chemistry, quantum natural language processing, and quantum AI.

CHAPTER 1

Introduction to Quantum Computing

Quantum computing is a rapidly growing field that works on the principle of quantum mechanics. In this chapter, we will discuss the prominent quantum mechanics concept with a bit of mathematical info and show how different fields came together to form a new field called *quantum*. We'll discuss some prominent gates and how to make a simple entangled state with a pictorial representation. Going through every concept of this chapter will prepare you to proceed to other concepts in later chapters.

Transition from Classical Physics to Quantum Physics

You can think of quantum physics and classical physics as two different game systems.

The game of checkers is classical physics. The game's rules are basic and uncomplicated, and it is obvious how each piece will go around the board. This is because of the way that classical physics represents the world in which we live, which is orderly and predictable. When you throw a ball, gravity pulls it back down to Earth. When you slide a book, friction causes it to stop. Simple, yes? This is what classical physics is all about!

Now, quantum physics is more like three-dimensional chess. It's not only more complicated, but the complexity has evolved. This doesn't mean the rules of checkers (classical physics) are wrong; they're just incomplete and different when we start playing checkers on a different kind of board, which is a 3D chessboard (on a microscopic level).

The universe of quantum physics is less intuitive. For example, a particle can be in two places at the same time until you measure it (like a chess piece that's both a pawn and a queen at the same time and decides what it is only when you look at it). This is known as *superposition*.

© Dhairyya Agarwal, Shalini D and Srinjoy Ganguly 2023
D. Agarwal et al., *Productizing Quantum Computing*, https://doi.org/10.1007/978-1-4842-9985-2_1

Or think about entanglement, another essential quantum physics idea. Imagine if shifting a single chess piece on your board instantly moved a piece on a board in another room. Strange, huh? However, in the quantum realm, particles are capable of being *entangled*, which means that no matter how far apart they are, the state of one particle is always tied to the state of another.

Similar to how learning the rules of checkers is a prerequisite for learning 3D chess, classical physics was necessary before quantum physics. However, the study of quantum physics allowed for a completely new understanding of how things (such as atoms and subatomic particles) function on a very small scale.

Therefore, scientists utilize classical physics to describe phenomena in our macro world and use quantum physics to explain phenomena at the micro level, just as you would use different techniques for playing checkers and 3D chess. Each set of guidelines has value and relevance within its own context.

A gradual transition from classical physics to quantum physics occurred during the early 20th century. There were a series of experiments done that paved the way for a separate, microscopic world called *quantum mechanics*. We will be discussing those experiments so you have a broad understanding of them. It's highly significant to know how these concepts were derived to gain an overall understanding of quantum computing (see Figure 1-1).

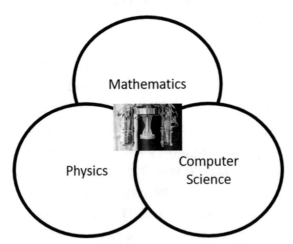

Figure 1-1. *The interdisciplinary nature of quantum computing requires knowledge of math, physics, and coding. Source: The quantum computer factory that's taking on Google and IBM | Yale Quantum Institute*

Fundamentals of Quantum Mechanics

When referring to the fundamental physics theory that describes how matter and energy behave at the smallest sizes, often at the level of atoms and subatomic particles, the phrases *quantum mechanics* and *quantum physics* are sometimes used interchangeably. Both names allude to the same field of study that aims to comprehend the nature of the universe at these scales, which has the potential to behave significantly differently from the classical world that we see in day-to-day life.

However, the term *quantum mechanics* frequently refers to a particular mathematical formalism or a set of guidelines used to describe quantum phenomena, whereas *quantum physics* may be used more broadly to refer to the study of physics when quantum effects are significant.

But both are used interchangeably.

Electromagnetic Spectrum

Electromagnetic spectrum is one of the interesting concepts you might be familiar with. This concept explains wavelength and frequency with respect to changes in energy. Let's take a quick glance at this concept (see Figure 1-2).

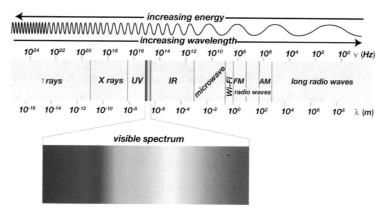

Figure 1-2. *Electromagnetic spectrum. Source: Why Do Sunsets On Mars Look Blue? » Science ABC*

The left side of the electromagnetic spectrum up until the visible spectrum represents radiations such as Gamma rays, X-rays, and UV rays. This radiation is dangerous and can cause numerous health hazards if exposed directly to the human body. These rays are considered dangerous because of their high frequency range. High frequency has higher energy, which makes the wavelength smaller, causing the radiation to be hazardous. On the other hand, the right side of the visible spectrum represents infrared radiation, microwaves, and radio waves. They have less frequency, which in turn has less energy, and a high wavelength makes the waves usable in daily life. For example, microwaves are used in our daily lives to heat food; radio waves transmit and receive signals, broadcast news, stream songs, etc.

The visible spectrum is what we call visible spectrum light. A crocodile can live both in water and on land. A human can survive in both summer and winter. In the same way, light can exist in two forms: wave and particle. Light behaves as a wave and a particle at the same time. Depending upon the experiments done to measure light, it will appear as a particle or a wave, even though it is actually both at the same time.

Planck's Constant

In an effort to explain blackbody radiation, Planck developed the idea of "quantization of energy." He postulated in 1900 that energy is quantized and can be released or absorbed only in discrete units, or *quanta*. The idea of the *quantum* was introduced as a result. This became the fundamental concept to explain quantum physics. The main theme of this concept is that "Energy is not continuous but discrete packets of light."

Consider yourself at a party where a vintage jukebox is providing the music. Only special coins can be used to play music on this one-of-a-kind jukebox. Each cent you insert entitles the jukebox to play a song for a predetermined, set period of time. You cannot insert a third of a coin or a half of a coin to play a third of a song or play half a song. There is just one coin for each unit of song time, neither more nor less.

In the universe of microscopic particles like atoms and photons (light particles), Planck's constant is comparable to the value of that particular coin. Energy doesn't come in any random quantity in the quantum universe; instead, it comes in predetermined "chunks" or "packets."

We don't see these chunks in our daily lives, just as you wouldn't hear individual notes in a song unless you pay very careful attention, because the value of this "coin" or packet size is very, very little (6.626×10^{-34} Joule seconds, to be precise). These pieces, however, matter a great deal on the atomic and subatomic scales.

Holistically, the size of the energy "coin" in the quantum jukebox is Planck's constant. It reveals that energy is quantized, or comes in fixed packets, at the most fundamental level, and this revelation altered our understanding of the cosmos at the tiniest scales.

$$E = h\nu$$

Here,

- E = Energy
- h = Planck's constant (6.626×10^{-34} Joule seconds)
- ν(nu) = Frequency

Uncertainty Principle

The Uncertainty Principle describes the uncertainty in position and momentum (speed) of an electron.

Imagine yourself as a guest at a darkly lit party with a spinning disco ball in the middle of the space. To record the movement and location of a specified area on the disco ball, you choose to use the phone's camera.

- *Trying to measure speed*: When attempting to measure speed, you would use a slower shutter speed or a longer exposure to try to catch the motion (speed) of the spot. A light streak that indicates motion will be seen, but because the light is moving, the exact location of the spot will be hazy.

- *Trying to measure position*: A quick shutter speed would be used to capture a clear image of the location at a certain time. By doing so, you may accurately record the spot's location without learning how quickly it is moving.

The more precisely you attempt to measure one aspect, such as position, the less precisely you can measure the other aspect, such as speed. A complete measurement of both cannot be obtained simultaneously.

This scenario of the party is somewhat analogous to Heisenberg's Uncertainty Principle in quantum physics. It asserts that it is impossible to accurately know both the position and the momentum of a particle, such as an electron, at the same time. The more accurately you understand one, the less accurately you understand the other.

This Uncertainty Principle also describes wave particle duality. When light acts as a wave, the momentum can be measured. When light behaves as a particle, the position can be measured.

As a product manager, you can compare the Uncertainty Principle with managing the development of a product. This requires frequently striking a balance between two important factors: speed and quality. The quality of the work could be compromised if you pressure your team to complete the task more quickly. On the other hand, your product launch could be delayed if you place too much emphasis on perfection. You can never completely eliminate uncertainty since it is impossible to accurately predict both speed and quality at the same time.

This is not because of some limitation in our measurement methods, but rather a fundamental property of quantum particles. The exact position and momentum of a quantum particle cannot be known at the same time, much as you cannot maximize speed and quality in product development.

Double Slit Experiment

This experiment describes the "wave nature of light."

Consider that you're testing a new website design and want to know how visitors use it. Consider installing two entryways (or *slits*) for users: doors A and B each lead to different features. It makes sense to assume that users will enter through either door. You can also keep tabs on exactly which features they are using by looking at both doors. In our comparison, this would be the corresponding result in classical physics.

Let's now introduce some quantum anomaly.

Scientists launch microscopic particles (such as electrons or photons) at a barrier with two slits in the double-slit experiment. In our analogy, if we consider these particles to be users, you expect them to pass through one slit or the other, just as consumers would choose between door A or door B.

The particles, however, were discovered by scientists to produce an interference pattern on the screen behind the barrier. The image on the screen shows that the particles are acting like waves and passing simultaneously through both slits, interfering with one another and producing a pattern of brilliant and dark patches.

Even if you're sending them in one at a time, in our website testing scenario, this would be like visitors somehow traveling through doors A and B at the same time, and their pathways would be interfering with one another to produce a pattern of high- and low-usage areas on your site.

The genuinely perplexing aspect is that the interference pattern vanishes if you try to determine which slit the particle passes through (much like trying to figure out which door the user entered)! The particles begin to behave as though they passed through only one slit, not both. This would be analogous to website visitors using only one door after you start keeping an eye on them.

This experiment demonstrates a fundamental principle of quantum mechanics: that the act of watching or measuring can really alter the behavior of particles. It's like our consumers start to act differently just because we're watching them—which, fortunately for you as a product manager, seldom happens in the macroscopic world in which we live!

Photo-electric Effect

The *photo-electric effect* refers to the particle nature of light. This means one can measure the position. You can assume a particle is an object that when thrown will have its position displaced. So, you can locate a particle but not a wave.

The photo-electric effect is comparable to a store's automated door sensor.

Imagine that you are in charge of a store and you have a sensor in place to detect when customers are approaching the entrance. The door opens when the sensor senses a consumer approaching (let's say when they are within a predetermined range). No matter how many people are outside the store, the door will remain closed if the customer is too far away.

In this case, the store is a metal surface, the customers are light (or more specifically, photons, which are tiny units of light), and the door is a representation of the metal's electrons.

A metal surface illuminated by light will resemble customers entering a store. It is possible to knock electrons (open the door) out of the metal if the light (customers) is of a high enough frequency or if the customers are close enough. The photo-electric effect looks like this.

Importantly, electrons are not knocked out until the light's frequency is high enough, just as the door doesn't open unless a customer is close enough. No matter how many people are standing outside the store or how much light shines on the metal, if the frequency isn't high enough, no electrons will be knocked out, and the door won't open.

This was an unexpected finding since it demonstrated wave-particle duality, the idea that light may behave like both a wave and a particle. Because it demonstrated the existence of discrete packets of light, known as *quanta*, as suggested by Planck and demonstrated by Einstein (who received the Nobel Prize for this explanation of the photo-electric effect), it also contributed to the quantum revolution.

De-Broglie Wavelength

You typically imagine a car as a substantial thing that can get you from one point to another. You wouldn't call it a "wave," would you? This is because a car's "wavelength" would be quite small and unnoticed in our daily lives.

Imagine if we could reduce the size of the car to the point where it is a subatomic particle, such as an electron. The automobile no longer just behaves like a particle at that tiny size; it also behaves like a wave, in accordance with quantum theory.

Physicist Louis de Broglie proposed what is now known as the *de Broglie hypothesis*, which suggests that matter has a dual nature. He suggested that waves can be found in all materials, not simply light. A straightforward calculation using Planck's constant and the particle's momentum, which is equal to the mass of the particle times its velocity, determines the "wavelength" of a particle (like our miniature automobile).

De Broglie essentially said that matter may behave both as a particle and as a wave, just like light. The wavelength of this matter-wave is denoted by the term *de Broglie wavelength*.

As a result, in the field of product management, it is possible to assert that just as a product can serve two purposes—for instance, a phone can also serve as a camera or as a GPS navigator—so can a particle, which can work as both a particle and a wave. One of the fundamental concepts upon which quantum physics is based is this wave-like motion, which becomes significant at extremely small scales.

All the previously mentioned experiments determined the wave particle duality and are foundational to quantum mechanics at all costs. Trying to have an idea is appreciable in the long run.

Transition from Quantum Physics to Quantum Computing

Max Planck, Albert Einstein, and Niels Bohr are some of the pioneers of quantum physics from the early 20th century. This is comparable to the early ideation stage of a product, when you are gathering ideas and developing the first basic prototypes.

Quantum physics had a solid reputation by the middle of the 20th century. Though they were largely using it in fields like nuclear physics and particle physics, scientists had a much better understanding of quantum mechanics. This is similar to the stage where you have a working prototype of your product but are unsure of how to market it or what its primary usage will be.

The connection of quantum with computation started during the 1980s, and Richard Feynmann took the ideas that were discussed around that time to mean that "Computation is a physical process merely a quantum mechanical one that in turn was questioned as how to compute (simulate) the physics." From here, he wanted to manifest the proposal of quantum computer that helped shaped the idea of quantum computing. This is the innovation or invention stage, when a ground-breaking new use for the technology is thought of. At present, we can say that quantum computing means computing done by governing the laws of quantum mechanical properties like superposition, interference, and entanglement.

Early in the new millennium, researchers began constructing the first basic quantum computers. In this stage of production, you build the first prototypes of a product and start to evaluate how it functions in practical settings.

The reliability and performance of quantum computers have greatly improved from the mid-2000s to the present, although they are still not ready for general use. This is comparable to the stage where you're perfecting a product, working out any bugs, and beginning to plan how to increase production.

Just like personal computers were in the 1970s or 1980s, the field of quantum computing is still developing and is thought to be in its early stages. Before quantum computers can be used by everyone, there are still a lot of obstacles to be solved, just like any cutting-edge product.

This was a condensed summary of the history, and it leaves out a lot of nuances and specifics. However, this section provided a broad overview of the development of quantum computing over the course of the 20th and 21st centuries.

The Need for Quantum Computing

In the early 20th century, the first transistor was developed. It was the size of a small hand, but as decades passed, millions of transistors were manufactured in a single chip that is less than a small finger and follows classical laws. We now think of those decades as the Silicon Era. Classical computers, made in accordance with the classical laws, are predominant now, and they're used in every possible industry ranging from education to scientific research. Classical computers are laptops, iPads, and computers that follow the classical laws of physics.

How do classical computers make use of classical laws of physics in their architecture?

- *Von Neumann architecture*: This framework defines how a computer's memory, processing unit, and input/output systems interact.

- *Follows Boolean logic*: The foundation of traditional computers is Boolean algebra, a mathematical framework that works with binary variables and logic operations such as AND, OR, and NOT.

- *Deterministic nature*: Since classical physics is inherently deterministic, it is possible to predict with 100 percent certainty what a system will do in the future if you fully understand its beginning conditions. Being based on fundamental physical principles, traditional computers are also deterministic, allowing for precise prediction of a computation's output based on its inputs.

- *Transistors*: Transistors, the fundamental components of digital circuits, are used in classical computers to produce logic gates. Classical electrical engineering ideas provide the foundation upon which transistors operate. They work by having two possible states, ON and OFF, which represent the binary numbers 1 and 0, respectively.

- *Signal transmission*: The transmission of signals in classical computers (electrical signals in wires) obeys classical electromagnetic laws, which have their origins in Maxwell's equation and Ohm's law.

- *Data storage*: Hard drives and solid-state drives (SSDs), two types of storage used in classical computers, function using concepts from electromagnetic and classical mechanics.

- *Materials and manufacturing*: The materials used in classical computer construction such as silicon, which is used in semiconductor devices, are based on the principles from classical physics including solid-state physics.

- *Error correction*: Errors that may arise during computation are corrected using classical error correction codes. These codes function according to the principles of classical information theory.

We have seen how classical laws of physics are used in every inch of classical computer architecture, but did you know that classical physics no longer works in quantum computer architecture?

How do quantum computers make use of quantum laws of physics?

Quantum computers are built and designed in accordance with quantum mechanics, which governs the behavior of matter and energy at small scales. Let's discuss fundamental quantum principles used to build and operate quantum computers.

- *Di Vincenzo's criteria*: Quantum computers were designed to meet certain criteria called *Di Vincenzo's criteria*. This criteria stresses the minimum requirements needed to build a functional quantum computer.

- *Probabilistic nature*: This defines the uncertainty associated with the measurement of a quantum system.

- *Encoding information*: Quantum computers may not necessarily use transistors but encode information into elementary particles such as electrons or photons.

- *Communication among qubits*: Interaction among qubits happens in a different way in different quantum systems. For example, in the superconducting systems, interaction happens via microwave resonators. In the trapped ion qubit systems, interaction happens via shared vibrational modes.

- *Data storage*: Auxiliary qubit states, which are used to hold data momentarily before it is employed in further phases of the algorithm, can be used to store interim outcomes during a quantum computation.

- *Quantum error correction*: Achieving noise-less quantum computers is the main challenge. Research is underway to develop fault-tolerant quantum computers. Quantum error correction codes are used that involve encoding a logical qubit into an entangled state.

So, we can understand that the major need for quantum computers is because of the exponential speedup and problem-solving nature for certain complex issues.

For example, consider yourself a product manager in the pharmaceutical industry tasked with developing a new drug. Developing novel medications entails sorting through millions of possible chemical combinations. Because of the enormous number of possible combinations to test, this process can take years, even with the fastest supercomputers. Quantum computers, on the other hand, have the potential to accelerate this process substantially. They have the potential to model and analyze chemical structures at a level of detail well beyond what traditional computers are capable of. This is considered a complexity in problem-solving.

Quantum Computing Basics

Think about a bag of sugar. Although the sugar can be poured out of the bag continuously, if you look closely, you can see that the sugar is actually made up of tiny individual grains. A grain of sugar cannot be divided into smaller pieces and still remain sugar since each grain is a separate, tiny object. Likewise, when Planck proposed the idea of quanta, he was arguing that energy, which had previously been perceived as something smooth and continuous (like a stream of water), was actually made up of tiny, distinctive "packets" (like the grains of sugar). These energy packets are the smallest form of energy that exists and cannot be further subdivided. This was a novel concept because it implied that energy wasn't as smooth and constant as previously believed in classical mechanics. It was instead "quantized," or divided into separate parts. One of the fundamental concepts that supports the discipline of quantum mechanics is this "quantum" notion of energy.

The reason for discrete amounts is because wave function and Schrodinger's equation, which are the mathematics of quantum mechanics, give rise to discrete or quantized values. You can consider more readily as the laws that govern the smaller particles (quantum physics) are different from the laws that govern larger particles (classical physics).

Quantum Bits (Qubits)

In classical computing, we call one unit of information a *bit*. Bits can be either 0 or 1 at a specific time. In the same way, a qubit means one unit of information and is different from classical mechanics because a qubit is in a superposition of 0 and 1. This superposition is because quantum objects (electrons or photons) show wave and particle nature (called wave-particle *duality*). This is like a quantum object that has two faces; one is a wave, and another is a particle. Depending upon the experiments done, either wave nature or particle nature is visible. We will discuss more about these experiments later.

Ways of Representing Qubits

There are different ways to represent a qubit. In the context of mathematical terms, a qubit can be represented in terms of *Dirac notation*. Dirac is the name of the scientist who pioneered quantum mechanics. Dirac notation has another name called *bra-ket notation*. Bra-ket represents the qubit state (quantum state) in terms of vector form. A vector is divided into row and column vectors. Ket is the notation used to represent a qubit state in terms of a column vector.

Bra notation is used to represent a qubit state in terms of row vectors. By default, ket notation (representation in terms of column vector form) is used.

If I say a qubit, you imagine I am talking about an electron/photon because quantum hardware uses electrons and photons as qubits. For convenience purposes, we can consider a qubit to be an electron. One of the properties of an electron is spin (intrinsic angular momentum). Electrons spin up and spin down, meaning *spin up* can be related to the 0 state and *spin down* can be related to the 1 state. Also, electrons can be in a superposition of up and down states. This superposition principle became the prominent reason to use electrons as qubits.

The 0 state can be represented as |0>0, which is called kept 0, and <0 | , which is called bra 0.

The 1 state can be written as |1> and called ket 1; <1| is called bra 1.

$$|0> = \begin{bmatrix} 1 \\ 0 \end{bmatrix}, \qquad |1> = \begin{bmatrix} 0 \\ 1 \end{bmatrix}$$

These are the mathematical representations of ket and bra for the 0 and 1 states. Ket notation is the transpose of bra notation.

In the context of computing, a Bloch sphere representation is used (Figure 1-3). A Bloch sphere is a visual tool to represent the state of a single qubit. The north pole of the Bloch sphere depicts |0> (Figure 1-4), and the south pole of the Bloch sphere depicts |1> (Figure 1-5). To make a transition from |0> to |1>, a rotation of 180° causes a transition of states. This rotation can be implemented with the help of quantum gates.

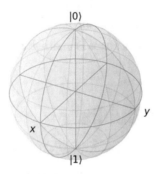

Figure 1-3. *Bloch sphere*

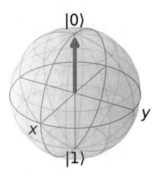

Figure 1-4. *Ket 0 state*

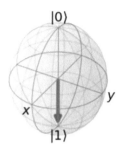

Figure 1-5. *Ket 1 state*

Measuring Qubit States

Let's represent the quantum state as $|\Psi\rangle$. The symbol $|\Psi\rangle$, pronounced "ket psi," is commonly used to denote a quantum state in the formalism of quantum mechanics known as Dirac, or bra-ket, notation. The wavefunction was a novel and crucial idea in the early stages of quantum mechanics, when the theory was being developed largely to describe the behavior of electrons in atoms. Psi (Ψ), a Greek letter, was chosen to symbolize it.

$\Psi(x,t)$ is a complex valued mathematical function, and its values are complex. *Complex values* means the equation has an imaginary part. For example, c = a+ib, where a = the real part, and ib = the complex part. The parameters of the wave function (x,t) depend upon the position, momentum, time, and spin of a quantum particle. For example, in a 1D quantum system, a wavefunction is a function of position and time: x = position and t = time. In the context of qubit, a wave function represents the state of a qubit $\Psi(x)$. Here, x is the state of a qubit.

The absolute square of a wavefunction $|\Psi(x)|^2$ equals the probability density of finding a quantum particle at a particular position x. This is known as the *Born rule*. The wave function isn't a physical object but a mathematical abstraction to predict the behavior of a quantum system. However, this is a crucial concept to predict the outcome of the quantum state once the measurement is done.

Ex: $|\Psi\rangle = \alpha|0\rangle + \beta|1\rangle$

Probability of $|0\rangle = |\alpha|^2$

Probability of $|1\rangle = |\beta|^2$

$|\alpha|^2 + |\beta|^2 = 1$

Here, we are taking an amplitude square that must be equal to 1.

Consider, $\alpha = \dfrac{1}{\sqrt{2}}$, $\beta = \dfrac{1}{\sqrt{2}}$.

$$\left|\dfrac{1}{\sqrt{2}}\right|^2 + \left|\dfrac{1}{\sqrt{2}}\right|^2 = 1.$$

Quantum Gates and Circuits

Quantum gates manipulate the bits of information. They act on qubits and change the state of a qubit. Gates are linear transformations themselves.

A collection of gates assigned according to the specificity of the qubits forms quantum circuits. You can consider quantum circuits as a collection of gates.

Figure 1-6 shows different types of quantum gates.

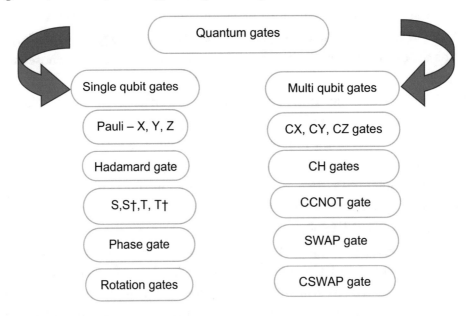

Figure 1-6. *Types of quantum gates*

Gates change the way the qubit should be. For example, if you have an X gate, which is also called a NOT gate, and it is applied to a qubit in the ket 0 state, the qubit state transforms to ket 1. There is a mathematical way to explain how qubits undergo transformations with the help of a matrix.

PAULI X GATE

This is also called a NOT gate. A bit flip occurs when an X gate is applied.

TRUTH TABLE

A truth table is a chart to help you understand the output of the system based on the input.

INPUT	OUTPUT
|0>	|1>
|1>	|0>

According to the representation of |0> and |1> and solving the vector form for it, you get the matrix representation of the X gate, and this step is followed for all other gates too.

$$X = \begin{bmatrix} 0 & 1 \\ 1 & 0 \end{bmatrix}$$

PAULI Y GATE

This is similar to the X gate, but an amplitude of "i" is multiplied by the output state. Here, a bit flip, as well as a phase flip, happens. The phase is flipped only if the input is in the |1> state.

TRUTH TABLE

INPUT	OUTPUT
|0>	i |1>
|1>	-i |0>

MATRIX

$$Y = \begin{bmatrix} 0 & -i \\ i & 0 \end{bmatrix}$$

PAULI Z GATE

The Z gate is also called the phase flip gate only when the input is in the | 1> state. But there is no bit flip.

TRUTH TABLE

INPUT	OUTPUT
|0>	|0>
|1>	-|1>

MATRIX

$$Z = \begin{bmatrix} 1 & 0 \\ 0 & -1 \end{bmatrix}$$

Differences Between Pauli Gates and Closest Classical Gates

The NOT gate is the Pauli-X gate's classical counterpart. The Pauli-Y and Pauli-Z gates don't have any classical equivalents, though. Pauli gates, for example, act on qubits in a superposition of states, whereas classical gates can affect bits only in a definitive state (0 or 1), enabling intricate transformations that are not feasible with classical gates.

Advantages Over Classical Gates

Pauli gates have the ability to influence the state of qubits in ways that classical gates cannot, such as entanglement and superposition. For some tasks, this results in the possibility of exponential speedups over traditional computers.

HADAMARD GATE

This is the most important and repeatedly used gate. This gate makes the qubit be in a superposition state. An H gate, along with a CX gate, creates entanglement. Once the H gate is applied, the qubit, which is in the |0> state, will be in a superposition of $|0> + |1>$, and $1/\sqrt{2}$ is the amplitude value, which, when magnitude is squared, results in 1/2. This is a 50 percent chance indicating the qubit will be in either $|0>$ or $|1>$.

TRUTH TABLE

INPUT	OUTPUT
|0>	$1/\sqrt{2} \ [\ |0> + |1>]$
|1>	$1/\sqrt{2} \ [\ |0> - |1>]$

MATRIX

$$H = \frac{1}{\sqrt{2}}\begin{bmatrix} 1 & 1 \\ 1 & -1 \end{bmatrix}$$

CX GATE

CX gate is a multiqubit (two) gate. This is also called a *controlled X gate*. A CX gate is precisely the same as an X gate, but the bit flip happens only with a condition. By default, the first qubit is a control qubit, and the second qubit is a target qubit. This can be changed according to our specifications in coding practices. If the control qubit is in the |1> state, the target qubit flips.

TRUTH TABLE

CONTROL QUBIT	TARGET QUBIT	OUTPUT
0	0	00
0	1	01
1	0	11
1	1	10

MATRIX

$$CX = \begin{bmatrix} 1 & 0 & 0 & 0 \\ 0 & 1 & 0 & 0 \\ 0 & 0 & 0 & 1 \\ 0 & 0 & 1 & 0 \end{bmatrix}$$

Quantum States and Superposition

We have seen that gates form linear transformations on states. But that state may not necessarily be in superposition. The superposition state is achieved only when the Hadamard gate is applied. We have seen the truth table and matrix form for the H gate.

In quantum computing, the superposition principle is a crucial idea. Superposition can be described as being in several places at once.

Consider that you own a coin. You won't know which side is up until you flip this coin; it might be either heads or tails. Even if we don't look at it, it is in one of these states in a classical world: heads or tails.

However, if this coin were a quantum particle, it could simultaneously be in both the heads and tails positions. It's not that we don't know which is true—it may be either one or the other. According to quantum theory, it truly is both at the same moment. The quantum coin "chooses" one of its states only when we measure it.

The following are the key takeaways from superposition:

- *Parallelism*: Since qubit states are both in 0 and 1, this allows quantum computers to perform calculations simultaneously. This makes the quantum computer have extraordinary computational speedups.

- *Entanglement*: Entanglement means we can know the state of one qubit by knowing the state of another irrespective of its distance. This concept is used in quantum cryptography.

- *Quantum algorithms*: Many quantum algorithms like Shor's and Grover's algorithms rely on superposition to achieve significant speedups over their classical counterparts.

Quantum Entanglement

Quantum superposition is a prerequisite to achieving entanglement. The property of one qubit will be known if another qubit is known, no matter at what distance it is. Say you have two dice; you are keeping one dice in a box and shipped to a distant island, but another is with you. When you open the box, you will know the number upright on the dice. You can say that other dice on the island also has the same number because they are entangled.

Figure 1-7 implements an entangled state. Quantum communication benefits heavily from this property.

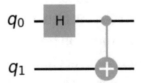

Figure 1-7. *A simple circuit showing the entangled property*

Summary

In this chapter, you learned about the classical physics transition to quantum physics, which says light has both wave and particle natures of light. You also learned about some prominent quantum mechanics concepts like Planck's constant, which describes the quantized nature of energy; the Uncertainty Principle, which describes that position and momentum can't be measured at the same time; the Double Slit experiment, which describes the wave nature of light; and the photo-electric effect experiment, which shows that when photons have energy, they kick the electrons out of a material proving the particle nature of light. De Broglie showed that even the tiniest of particle can behave as a wave-like pattern. The transition from quantum physics to quantum computing stemmed from a proposal from Richard Feynmann. The importance of quantum computing is because of the runtime efficiency and the ability to solve problems that classical laws of physics take years to compute or are unable to do. A qubit is one unit of information. There are different ways of representing qubits, which were explained in detail. Measuring qubits gives a certain output (state). Quantum gates are the linear transformation acting on the qubit causing the state to transform and the output state to be different. For the beginner purposes, we looked at only Pauli gates and two-qubit gates. Superposition allows the quantum states to be in multiple states at once. If the particles are entangled, then we can know the properties of one state if another state is known.

CHAPTER 2

Quantum Algorithms and Applications

In the previous chapter, we discussed the basics of quantum computing and some essential properties such as superposition, entanglement, and the Uncertainty Principle. In this chapter, we will discuss a few prominent quantum algorithms and their applications.

Introduction to Quantum Algorithms

A remarkable fusion of computer science, quantum physics, and pure inventiveness results in quantum algorithms. They provide us with a tantalizing peek into the future when we will be able to tackle complicated issues more quickly and effectively than we ever could with conventional computers. What, then, is so unique about quantum algorithms? Let's revisit some concepts quickly.

A qubit can be both a 0 and a 1 at the same time, unlike a traditional bit that can be only one or the other. We refer to this "being in two places at once" as a *superposition*. Imagine a juggler who can handle several balls at once. Similar to that, superposition enables a quantum computer to manage many calculations at once. The rules governing this process are quantum algorithms, which enable quantum computers to handle massive volumes of data at a breakneck pace.

Entanglement, another quantum property discussed earlier, increases the plot's complexity. The property of one qubit affects the property of another qubit regardless of their distance from one another. With the help of superposition and entanglement properties, quantum algorithms open up the world of possibilities for secure and faster communication.

© Dhairyya Agarwal, Shalini D and Srinjoy Ganguly 2023
D. Agarwal et al., *Productizing Quantum Computing*, https://doi.org/10.1007/978-1-4842-9985-2_2

The potential of quantum algorithms is what makes them beautiful. Shor's and Grover's algorithms, which exponentially speed up factoring big numbers and expediate searching through an unsorted database, respectively, are the tip of the quantum iceberg. These algorithms have the potential to completely change a variety of industries, including machine learning, data science, optimization, and cryptography.

But bear in mind that the revolution in quantum computing is still in its infancy. Scalability and error correction are major obstacles for quantum computers and algorithms, but the potential rewards are enormous.

Every quantum algorithm has a specific way of solving a computational problem. Quantum algorithms (see Figure 2-1) are represented in terms of quantum circuits, which consist of quantum gates. The number of quantum gates can affect the runtime. Also, the runtime depends upon several other factors such as optimization, error rates, parallelism, and the nature of quantum hardware design.

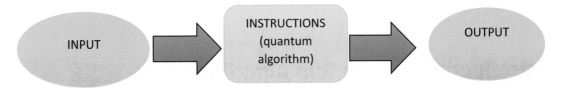

Figure 2-1. *How a quantum algorithm works*

Designing Quantum Algorithms

We will see the basic design of quantum algorithms. These are the common steps in every algorithm design:

- *Understanding the problem*: If you want to search unsorted data, consider what inputs are to be given and what outputs you need to get.

- *Designing the quantum circuit*: Decide on the number of qubits needed for the proposed problem.

- *Initializing the state*: By default, qubits are initialized to ket 0. But, depending upon the complexity of problems, the qubits initialization can be changed.

- *Operating gates*: Quantum gates manipulate states. Gates can be single-qubit or multiqubit gates.

- *Measuring qubits*: Once a quantum state is manipulated with gates, states are measured.

- *Verifying the algorithm*: The algorithms are tested and verified using quantum simulators, and the necessary improvements are done once verified.

How Efficient Are Quantum Algorithms Compared to Their Classical Counterparts?

Usually, the efficiency of quantum algorithm is determined by two methods.

- Runtime

- Big-O

Runtime

The runtime is the amount of computer time it takes to execute an algorithm. For example, consider an athlete sprinter in the Olympics who recorded 100-meter relay in 10.3 seconds. This is the runtime of an athlete. In the same way, how fast an algorithm can deliver its output is related to the runtime. But, the runtime depends upon the number of gates used and its complexity.

Big-O

The worst-case scenario for how an algorithm's runtime can increase in relation to the size of the input is represented by Big-O notation.

This also compares the efficiency of quantum algorithms with their classical counterparts.

- *O(1), constant time*: The operation's execution time is constant regardless of the size of the input. An illustration would be using the element's index to retrieve it in an array.

- *O(log n), logarithmic time*: The time it takes to complete the operation grows logarithmically with the size of the input. A binary search in a sorted array is a perfect example of this.

- $O(\sqrt{n})$, *square root*: The algorithm's complexity roughly increases with the square root of the input size.

- $O(n)$, *linear*: The runtime increases linearly with the input size. An example is a simple "for" loop processing each element of an array once.

- $O(n \log n)$, *linear logarithmic time*: The runtime increases proportionally to n log n. Many efficient sorting algorithms such as heapsort and merge sort exhibit this time complexity.

- $O(n^2)$, *quadratic time*: The runtime increases in proportion to the square of input size. Bubble sort is an example.

- $O(2^n)$, *exponential time*: The runtime doubles with each addition to the input data set. This is common in many brute-force algorithms.

- $O(n!)$, *factorial time*: This is one of the least effective complexities and is frequently linked to computation-intensive methods, including brute-force search algorithms that attempt all possible combinations of a collection of data.

See Figure 2-2.

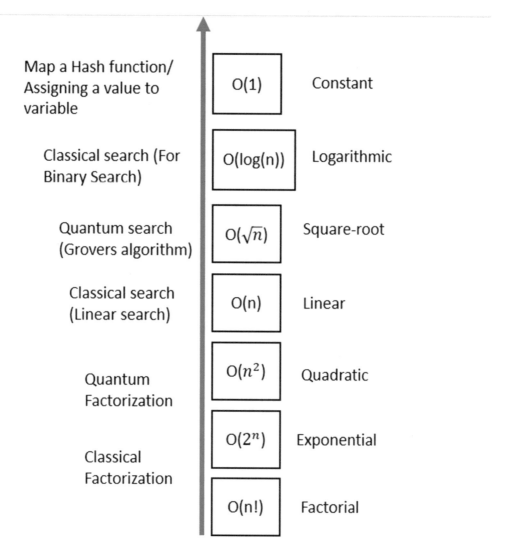

Figure 2-2. *Big-notation comparison*

Let's discuss a few prominent quantum algorithms in detail.

Shor's Algorithm

Peter Shor in 1996 discovered the Shor's algorithm, which is considered to be significantly better than classical algorithms. The main reason for such a big statement is because of its time complexity. Time complexity is represented by Big-O notation.

Shor's algorithm is designed to factorize large integers.

Classical Algorithm for Factorization

The simplest conventional factorization algorithm is trial division, which involves trying to divide the number by all integers up to its square root. The complexity in terms of time is $O(\sqrt{N})$, where N is the number that needs to be factored. This is too slow for really large numbers.

The general number field sieve, the best known classical algorithm for factoring large integers, has a time complexity of roughly $O(e^{1.9(\log\log N)^{1/3}(\log\log\ \log\log N)^{2/3}})$, where N is the number of bits in the number to be factored.

This classical algorithm is too slow for large number factorization. This is the reason Shor's algorithm is considered to be the more efficient one.

Shor's Algorithm for Integer Factorization

Shor's algorithm runs in polylogarithmic time, indicating that the time required is polynomial in relation to the input's size. There is no precise time complexity available owing to the lag of quantum hardware advancement. With recent advancements, Shor's time complexity goes until $72(\log N)^3$. Thy is the integer factorization prominent? This is due to the applications in different industries.

- *Cryptography*: One of the most widely used public-key cryptography systems is the RSA (Rivest-Shamir-Adleman) algorithm, which relies heavily on the difficulty of factoring large integers. In RSA, the public key is a product of two large prime numbers, and the private key is derived from the factors of the public key. If an efficient algorithm for factoring large integers were to be discovered (or if a large-scale quantum computer capable of running Shor's algorithm were to be built), it would break RSA and necessitate the development of new cryptographic algorithms. This has led to a lot of interest in post-quantum cryptography, which is cryptography that would remain secure even in the presence of a large-scale quantum computer.

- *Number theory*: A fundamental operation in number theory, a discipline of pure mathematics devoted to the study of integers, is factoring. Numerous number-theoretic issues can be resolved, and new mathematical theories can be developed by having a solid understanding of integer factorization.

Applications of Shor's Algorithm

There are a number of common applications of Shor's algorithm.

- *Breaking RSA cryptography*: The ability of Shor's algorithm to defeat RSA encryption is perhaps its most well-known use. A popular public-key cryptosystem for safe data transmission is RSA encryption. It is based on the notion that factoring huge numbers is challenging and that there is no known effective classical algorithm for this problem. However, RSA encryption becomes vulnerable if large-scale quantum computers become feasible and are able to execute Shor's algorithm.

- *Study of number theory*: The study of integers and integer-valued functions is the focus of the pure mathematics discipline of number theory, which could benefit from Shor's algorithm.

- *Cryptanalysis*: In addition to RSA, other cryptographic systems, including elliptic-curve cryptography, rely on the difficulty of specific mathematical puzzles. A quantum computer executing Shor's algorithm might be able to solve these issues if they can be reduced to factorization (or discrete logarithms).

Grover's Search Algorithm

The Grover search algorithm was developed by Lov Grover in 1996. This algorithm is used for unsorted database search.

Classical Algorithm for Unsorted DB Search

Imagine you have a deck of cards. You want one particular card out of all 52 cards. In classical computing, in the worst case, every card will be gone through (or by hand), which has a time complexity of $O(N)$ queries, where N is the size of the database. This is a daunting process if the number of cards are multiplied.

This daunting process will be drastically reduced by introducing Grover's search algorithm. The time complexity taken to do an unsorted database search is $O(\sqrt{N})$, where N is the size of the database. The main reason for this speedup is utilizing quantum mechanical properties such as the following:

- *Superposition*: All the states are initialized to a superposition state. The main reason for the success of Grover's technique is the ability to do parallel computing. Multiple tasks can be done in parallel. Consider the card example; by utilizing Grover's search, multiple cards can be looked at once.

- *Quantum interference*: Another important component that is utilized in Grover's technique is quantum interference. The fact that quantum particles (electrons, photons) behave like waves is what causes interference. The probabilities of quantum states can also interfere, just like waves in a pond can do so either constructively (by adding up) or destructively (by canceling out). For Grover's algorithm, we want the "correct" answer's probability to constructively interfere (raise), while the "incorrect" answer's probability to destructively interfere (drop). This process is accomplished by applying Grover's diffusion operator repeatedly, increasing the probability of measuring the right response.

- *Amplitude amplification*: This is the key technique in Grover's algorithm. Amplitude amplification increases the amplitude of the correct state and decreases the amplitude of the incorrect state. (*Amplitude* means height of the wave or strength of the quantum state, and *amplification* means increasing the height of the wave or strength of the quantum state.) In this way, the correct item is identified from the unsorted database by amplifying the correct item's probabilities. Once measured, the correct item is identified with maximum probability (but not 100 percent certainty).

Possible Applications of Grover's Search Algorithm

There are a couple of possible applications of Grover's search algorithm.

- *Quantum simulation*: In some quantum simulations, since the goal is to select a particular state from a huge pool of potential states that fits certain requirements, Grover's approach can be utilized as a subroutine.

- *Machine learning*: Grover's approach can be used in the area of quantum machine learning to accelerate certain tasks. It can be used, for instance, to shorten the training period for specific classifier types.

- *Cryptography*: By halving the key size, Grover's approach can be used to accelerate the discovery of a cryptographic key during a brute-force attack. For this reason, post-quantum cryptography concentrates on cryptographic algorithms that would continue to function securely even in the presence of quantum computers that could execute Grover's algorithm.

Variational Quantum Algorithm

The term *variational* is a method/classical technique used in quantum mechanics to estimate the ground state of a quantum system.

The ground state of a quantum system is the lowest energy state according to quantum physics. As a pendulum hangs straight down while it is not swinging, the system can be thought of as being at "rest" and doing nothing. Every possible state of the system has a certain amount of energy, and the ground state is the state with the least energy.

Purpose to Estimate the Ground State?

This is because the system's ground state provides crucial information, such as its stability and behavior at low temperatures. For instance, in quantum chemistry, comprehending a molecular system's ground state can reveal important details about chemical reactivity and bonding. The quantum algorithm called the *variational quantum eigensolver* (VQE) was created specifically for this need.

By maximizing a cost function, variational quantum algorithms can be employed in quantum machine learning to train quantum neural networks. One way to describe this procedure is "finding the ground state" of a quantum system, where the neural network and cost function define the system.

Some popular examples of VQA include variational quantum eigensolver (VQE) and quantum approximate quantization algorithm (QAOA). These algorithms leverage classical and quantum resources to solve a variety of problems, especially when only noisy, intermediate-scale quantum (NISQ) computers are available.

NISQ stands for noise-intermediate scale quantum. This term was coined by John Preskill, and it describes the next few generations of quantum computers we expect to build.

There are two features of NISQ computers.

- *Intermediate scaling*: These quantum computers will have a few dozen to several hundred, or perhaps even several thousand, qubits. Large-scale quantum computers, on the other hand, would have tens of thousands or perhaps millions of qubits.

- *Noisy*: The qubits in these devices are not perfect and can be easily disturbed or "decohered" by their environment. This leads to errors in the computation. The term *noisy* refers to this high error rate.

NISQ computers are not targeted to achieve "quantum supremacy" but to target specific potential applications. Variational quantum algorithms like variational quantum eigensolver (VQE) and quantum approximation optimization algorithm (QAOA) , which are hybrid quantum-classical algorithms, are particularly suited to NISQ computers.

Variational Quantum Eigensolver

VQE is used to find the ground-state energy of a molecule. VQE is considered to be a hybrid algorithm because VQE involves quantum and classical computations. Eigensolver means finding the eigenvalues and its eigenvectors for a given matrix or operator.

Importance of Finding Eigenvalues

In simpler terms, consider an eigenvalue as a distinctive characteristic or identification of a system, similar to a barcode or QR code on a product. Any important details about a product, such as its price, maker, when it was created, etc., are provided when its barcode is scanned. Similar to this, determining a system's eigenvalue provides important details about that system's behavior. Eigenvalues frequently refer to the energy levels of quantum states in the context of quantum computing. It is comparable to knowing the energy cost for each possible condition for a system. Many different fields require this knowledge.

In quantum chemistry, for example, understanding the eigenvalue (energy level) of a molecule's ground state, or lowest energy configuration, can reveal an array of information about the molecule's characteristics, including how it will interact with other molecules. Similar to this, the objective of quantum algorithms like quantum phase estimation is to determine the eigenvalue of a unitary operator, which offers important details about the system to which it is applied.

In light of the fact that eigenvalues are a component of the crucial data your quantum products or services will deal with, the idea of eigenvalues is important to you as a product manager. Understanding them can improve your understanding of the advantages and future uses of quantum technologies.

Applications of VQE

The following are applications of VQE:

- *Quantum chemistry*: Protein folding and drug discovery using molecular combination

- *Finance*: Portfolio optimization and risk management

- *Transport*: In-route optimization and traveling salesman problem

- *Molecular simulation*: Discovering optimizations in carbon capture, alternative renewable resources, and battery design

Quantum Machine Learning

At the nexus of machine learning (ML) and quantum physics, there is a rapidly expanding interdisciplinary topic called *quantum machine learning* (QML). To address challenging computational issues that are unsolvable by conventional computers, it aims to combine the strength of quantum computing with the promise of machine learning approaches.

Think of a typical machine learning process as a classroom setting with students. You hand a book (the data) to the student (the algorithm). The student gains information from this book, and their understanding grows with each new book (of data) they read.

But what if there are too many books (big data) and the books are in another language? The pupil can take too long or not learn anything at all. The "curse of dimensionality," which refers to the fact that as a dataset's dimensionality (number of features) increases, the volume of the data expands exponentially and becomes more difficult to manage and analyze, might limit the performance of machine learning algorithms.

Quantum machine learning can help in this situation. It's comparable to giving our student a quantum computer with superhuman brain capacity. The learning process is sped up by this superbrain's capacity to read numerous books simultaneously (parallel computations) and even comprehend complex languages (handle complex data). It is possible for quantum computers to process information more effectively than classical computers by using quantum mechanical phenomena such as superposition and entanglement. Theoretically, they could handle high-dimensional data and carry out parallel computations at speeds that are faster than those possible with traditional systems.

Quantum versions of well-known machine learning methods, including quantum principal component analysis (QPCA) and quantum support vector machines (QSVM), have been proposed and investigated. The plan is to use quantum operations to process the data and derive information after encoding it into quantum states, also referred to as qubits.

Don't get ahead of yourself, though. The field of quantum machine learning is still developing. Quantum computers that can outperform classical ones are not yet readily accessible. It appears as though our superbrain is still in the planning stages. The great promise it possesses, however, is unaffected by the early difficulties, just like with any ground-breaking technology.

Our approach to handling massive data and complicated issues may be completely changed by quantum machine learning. It might have an effect on areas including artificial intelligence, weather forecasting, financial modeling, and medication discovery. Understanding the possibilities and implications of quantum machine learning can be crucial for you as a product manager. It's like gaining a front-row seat to the potential future of business and technology.

The game may change when the quantum revolution in machine learning does come to pass. The visionaries will set themselves apart from others by anticipating this transformation and preparing for it. Being at the cutting edge of this revolutionary technology will provide you with the tools necessary to lead your team and your goods into a future dominated by quantum machine learning.

To understand quantum machine learning in a better way, we describe the QSVM algorithm in a simplified manner here:

- *Data encoding*: Data encoding, sometimes referred to as data embedding or feature mapping, is the initial phase. This process involves converting classical data into a quantum state. To represent the data in a way that is challenging, if not impossible, to achieve with classical systems, this encoding makes use of quantum features such as superposition and entanglement. Simply explained, this stage entails converting a data set into a language that the quantum computer can efficiently interpret and manipulate.

- *Quantum processing*: Quantum processing is the following step after the data has been put into a quantum state. Here, the quantum data is manipulated using quantum gates, which are the fundamental building blocks of quantum processing. The core of a quantum machine learning algorithm's computation process is formed by these gates, which together form a "quantum circuit." Based on the quantum mechanical concepts of superposition, entanglement, and interference, this circuit modifies the quantum data's state.

- *Measurement*: The last phase is measurement, which comes after quantum processing. The quantum state is monitored here after going through the quantum circuit. The quantum state in quantum mechanics "collapses" to one of its potential outcomes during the measurement process, giving us a classical readout. The probabilistic nature of quantum physics, however, may necessitate repeated measurements to obtain accurate results.

- *Classical post-processing*: The results may require some additional post-processing after the quantum data has been measured and transformed back into classical data. Standard methods from conventional machine learning can be used in this post-processing to enhance and explain the quantum system's initial output.

- *Learning and iteration*: Algorithms for quantum machine learning are iterative by design. The quantum circuit is improved, and the precision of the results is increased using the data from the first iteration of the procedure. The process is continued until the best solution is identified.

Applications of Quantum Machine Learning

The following are the applications of quantum machine learning.

- *Artificial intelligence and big data*: AI could significantly advance with the help of quantum machine learning, especially when it comes to handling huge and complex data sets. This might make it possible to create more complex AI models and draw valuable conclusions from massive amounts of data.

- *Climate modeling*: The speed and precision of climate models could be dramatically increased by quantum machine learning. These models are frequently intricate and computationally demanding. Quantum computers' enhanced processing power may enable more precise and thorough climate predictions.

- *Drug discovery*: To treat diseases, the pharmaceutical industry is continuously in search of innovative medication ingredients. It takes a lot of searching through a huge space of probable molecules to find these compounds. This technique can be aided by quantum machine learning, which can greatly increase the effectiveness of the search and possibly find new medications that conventional methods might have overlooked. This might also lead to personal medicine developments wherein a patient can be more easily matched directly to the best drug that would fight their particular illness.

- *Supply chain optimization*: To maintain effective operation, supply networks must be optimized by balancing a variety of factors. These large and complicated datasets may be processed more quickly and accurately with quantum machine learning, which could result in more effective supply chains and lower operational costs.

Other Quantum Algorithms and Applications

The following are some other algorithms.

Deutsch Jozsa Algorithm

The Deutsch Jozsa algorithm was developed by David Deutsch and Richard Jozsa in 1992. This algorithm was the earliest of all advanced algorithms such as Grover's, Shor's etc., and it was developed to demonstrate the quantum computer outperformance over classical algorithms. This proved to outperform in specific tasks. But this is not a practically implemented one. Still, Deutsch Jozsa is a theoretical framework, but it showed quantum supremacy in earlier stages.

Quantum Phase Estimation

Quantum phase estimation (QPE) has an ability to estimate the eigenvalues of a unitary operator. QPE itself is an algorithm that is used in many algorithms.

Consider a "unitary operator" as a kind of magic box that, when something is put into it, modifies things in certain ways. Consider a box that doubles anything you put in it. Two apples would result from the insertion of one apple.

This box has a certain quality known as a *eigenvalue*. Continuing with our example, the eigenvalue can be "2" because anything you put into this box always doubles.

Currently, QPE acts as a detective by determining this characteristic (eigenvalue) of the magic box (unitary operator) without requiring you to open the box and examine what is inside. It starts with a good guess and improves it until it's as exact as it can be.

The phrase "QPE itself is an algorithm that is used in many algorithms" refers to the fact that this detective (QPE) is useful for more than deciphering the workings of magic boxes (unitary operators). It's a useful tool that may be applied in numerous contexts to address a range of issues. Similar to how a detective may be hired to assist with various types of investigations, other algorithms can incorporate QPE as part of their operations.

Understanding QPE is similar to having a tool in your toolbox that can help you identify particular traits of complicated systems in the context of your job as a product manager. This tool can be especially helpful when creating quantum algorithms and forecasting their behavior.

Applications of QPE in Other Algorithms

These are other applications:

- *Shor's algorithm*: This is used to factorize large integers by an exponentially faster method than classical method. Shor's algorithm uses QPE to find the period of function, which in turn identifies the factors of numbers.

- *Quantum simulation*: Utilizing a quantum system (such as a quantum computer) to model another quantum system is known as quantum simulation.

  Consider a metropolis, let's name it Quantumville, that is populated by skyscrapers of various heights. The height of the skyscraper corresponds to the energy of each of the several states that a quantum system might be in.

  Now, in this metropolis, there is a very specific rule: the higher the tower, the more expensive the rent is. Everyone is attempting to live in the smallest building possible because it is the most affordable. The "ground state" of our quantum system is analogous to this shortest building; it is the one with the lowest energy or cost. But Quantumville is a huge city, not a tiny town. There are so many skyscrapers there that it would take an eternity to count them all and determine which one is the shortest. This is comparable to how a classical computer finds it difficult to determine the ground state of a complicated quantum system because it must investigate a vast array of potential outcomes, which can take a very long period.

  Imagine a superhero—let's name them Quantum Phase Estimator (QPE)—who could fly over the city and locate the shortest skyscraper considerably faster than anyone could by manually inspecting each building. QPE has the ability to swiftly and accurately estimate the states of the quantum system, or the height of the buildings, or the energy level in quantum terms.

- *HHL algorithm*: This is a quantum machine learning algorithm that solves a system of linear equations on a quantum computer. The HHL algorithm uses QPE to estimate the eigenvalues of a system matrix.

Quantum Approximate Optimization Algorithm

Using a quantum computer, the *quantum approximate optimization algorithm* (QAOA) is a hybrid quantum-classical technique for combinatorial optimization issues. Because it does not require error correction, which is currently one of the major hurdles in the industry, it is one of the most promising methods for deploying near-term quantum devices.

The fundamental goal of QAOA is to produce a quantum state that, when measured, offers an effective solution to the specified optimization problem. By building a parameterized quantum circuit that transforms an initial state into a final state, this is accomplished. The circuit's characteristics are then classically tuned to improve the chances of obtaining an accurate measurement.

Applications of QAOA

These are some applications:

- *Traveling salesman problem (TSP)*: This well-known optimization problem asks for the quickest path a salesperson on the road should take to stop in several places before returning to the starting point. It is a possible target for quantum computing techniques like QAOA because it is an NP-hard issue. NP stands for "nondeterministic polynomial time."

- *Portfolio optimization*: A crucial issue in finance is how to distribute wealth among various assets to optimize projected returns and reduce risk. This can be written as a QAOA-compatible quadratic optimization problem.

- *Vehicle routing problem*: This is similar to the TSP, but with more intricate constraints and numerous cars. Applications are widely used in supply chain management and logistics.

- *Max cut problem*: This entails dividing a graph's nodes into two groups in a way that maximizes the number of edges between the groups. Applications include VLSI design in computer engineering and community discovery in social networks.

- *Drug discovery*: To determine a molecule's minimal energy conformation or to resolve the protein folding conundrum, QAOA can be used in biochemistry and pharmacology. Both drug discovery and materials science may benefit from this.

Implementing Quantum Algorithms in Quantum Computers

These are some implementations:

- Scientists have implemented a "complete three-qubit Grover search algorithm with greater performance than classical, employing scalable quantum computing technology of trapped atomic ions."

- In 2001, IBM demonstrated an early kind of quantum computer called a liquid state nuclear magnetic resonance quantum computer to successfully factor the number 15.

Note   Since quantum algorithms and quantum hardware are in their developmental stage, there is not much data available about them.

Challenges and Limitations of Quantum Algorithms

These are some of the challenges:

- *Error correction*: Decoherence, a phenomena that can quickly shatter delicate quantum states, is a result of environmental noise. Quantum calculations are hence prone to mistakes. Although there are theoretical approaches for error correction, they have a high overhead in terms of qubits and processing power.

- *Fault tolerance*: Because of the intrinsic instability of quantum states, a quantum computer must be able to carry out calculations even in the presence of errors to be useful. Research on fault-tolerant quantum computing is still going on.

- *Intersecting knowledge*: A knowledge of quantum mechanics is necessary for the new and complicated discipline of quantum programming. More reliable and approachable quantum programming languages and environments are required.

Choosing the Right Quantum Algorithm for Your Business

Here is how to choose the right algorithm for you:

- *For quantum chemistry research*: VQE can be the best choice if your company is working in the field of quantum chemistry, where complicated chemical and molecular reactions are modeled and understood at a quantum level. Why? Because VQE is designed primarily to ascertain the energy of a molecule's ground state. For complicated molecules, traditional computational methods can be time- and resource-intensive, sometimes taking days to weeks. To potentially attain these results in a shorter amount of time, VQE makes use of the quantum features of superposition and entanglement. This has the potential to dramatically speed up research and development in the fields of material science, drug discovery, and other chemistry-related fields.

- *To solve optimization problems*: The QAOA could be a game-changer for businesses dealing with complicated optimization challenges, whether they are related to scheduling work, resource allocation, or logistics optimization. These issues frequently get exponentially more complex as the number of variables rises, making it practically difficult to resolve them by conventional methods. QAOA works by converting the optimization issue into a quantum state and then applying quantum mechanics to discover approximations of the answers. This strategy may result in significant speedups, enabling companies to find better solutions more quickly and effectively than using conventional algorithms.

- *For quantum finance research*: In the field of finance, enormous amounts of data are examined to inform critical choices, identify patterns, and improve portfolios. The following quantum algorithms are recommended for the reasons listed next.

- *HHL algorithm*: The HHL method is something to take into account if your company is looking to solve huge systems of linear equations, which frequently appear in risk assessment, pricing, and various optimization problems in finance. Financial firms may process and analyze huge datasets with increased efficiency thanks to their promised exponential speedups over conventional methods.

- *QAE algorithm*: QAE offers a competitive advantage for activities such as option pricing, which includes estimating specific probabilistic outcomes. This algorithm is intended to provide speedier and more accurate pricing options and risk assessments by estimating specific quantities with fewer resources than conventional techniques.

Summary

In this chapter, we discussed quantum algorithms and their efficiency over classical algorithms. Here, efficiency is related to the runtime, which is better than classical algorithms. The best examples are Shor's algorithm, Grover's search algorithm, and variational quantum algorithms. We also discussed their possible applications. Quantum machine learning is a separate domain that has multiple uses, and active research is going on in this field. A few other algorithms like Deutsch Jozsa, quantum phase estimation, and the quantum approximation optimization algorithm were also discussed in detail. This was not a complete list of quantum algorithms, but we covered the ones that have prominence and active research development going on. There are other algorithms like Deutsch, Bernstein Vazirani, and Simon's algorithm that don't have many applications yet.

CHAPTER 3

Introduction to Quantum Computers

In this chapter, we will discuss the types of quantum computers and their advantages and disadvantages.

Quantum Computers

Quantum computers use quantum mechanical properties such as superposition, entanglement, and quantum interference to deliver huge leaps in processing power. Quantum machines promise to outrun even the most capable of today's and tomorrow's supercomputers.

This doesn't pose any threat to the classical computers we use for our daily use. In fact, classical computers are the easiest and economical to build. But quantum computers promise to advance various fields ranging from material sciences to pharmaceuticals research. The main reason for this supremacy is that quantum computers are able to simulate the behavior of matter down to a molecular level. Companies began to experiment with them when trying to develop lighter and more powerful batteries for electric cars and novel drugs. A few auto manufacturers are using quantum computers to simulate the chemical composition of electrical vehicle batteries to improve their performance. Quantum computing with the intersection of machine learning created a new field called *quantum machine learning*. In the future, if we can develop a fault-tolerant quantum computer, then quantum machine learning possesses a huge market and has its own opportunities.

The secret to a quantum computer's power is the ability to generate and manipulate qubits. We discussed qubits in detail in Chapter 1. The type of quantum algorithms used determines the efficiency of a quantum computer along with the type of hardware used. We discussed popular quantum algorithms in detail in Chapter 2.

D. Agarwal et al., *Productizing Quantum Computing*, https://doi.org/10.1007/978-1-4842-9985-2_3

Types of Quantum Computers

Figure 3-1 shows the types of quantum computers.

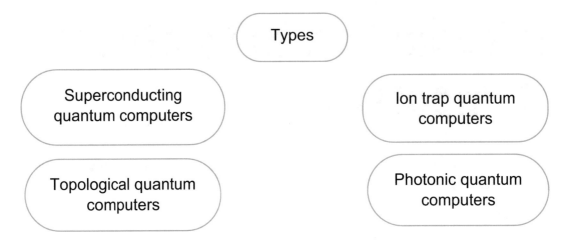

Figure 3-1. *Types of quantum computers*

Superconducting Quantum Computers

Imagine yourself in a city where the sole route from your home to your place of business is a straight path, and you travel using a standard automobile that can travel one location at a time. This situation is comparable to a traditional computer, which can process only one item simultaneously, similar to driving straight.

Imagine having a magic automobile at this point. This vehicle can teleport, fly, and simultaneously move between numerous locations along roadways. Suddenly, you can leave your house and immediately go to the office, the grocery store, and the gym. This situation is comparable to a quantum computer, which can process enormous amounts of data concurrently.

Imagine that only cities with subzero temperatures—colder than Antarctica—can use this fantastic car. You can compare the previous climate to a superconducting quantum computer. These computers need frigid circumstances with temperatures near absolute zero to preserve their "magic" abilities.

Your magic automobile needs a special engine with rapid start/stop for the cold city. These engines are analogous to the qubits in a superconducting quantum computer, which are tiny circuits that can maintain their quantum state for as long as they are kept extremely cold.

In short, a superconducting qubit is a tunable electrical circuit that behaves like an artificial atom. The circuit can carry current at very low temperatures without any resistance. The circuit uses a Josephson junction, which is a superconducting device that allows current to tunnel across them.

Advantages of Superconducting Quantum Computers

Here are few advantages of superconducting quantum computers:

- *Efficiency*: Superconductors are substances that, at very low temperatures, enable electricity to flow without encountering any resistance. This is comparable to having a water channel that transmits water without losing even a single drop. This implies that we can have extremely effective computations with little information loss in quantum computing. In other words, these devices will operate more effectively while using less electricity.

- *Interconnection with existing technology*: Superconducting circuits are designed by the micro/nanofabrication methods, which are normally used to design classical chips.

- *Less loss of information*: Minimal loss of information occurs due to the presence of Cooper pairs because Cooper pairs flow through the crystal lattice without resistance. *Cooper pairs* means a pair of electrons. One of the primary explanations for why superconductors can carry electricity so well is because of these pairs of electrons, which pass through a superconductor without encountering any resistance.

Disadvantages of Superconducting Quantum Computers

These are the disadvantages:

- *Lower coherence time*: The duration of a qubit in a quantum system to retain its quantum state without significant loss/decoherence is called coherence time. This is <300 µs. The difficulty of having high coherence time increases with the increase in qubits.

- *Interaction*: Coupling in 2D geometrics is restricted only to nearby qubits. Superconducting qubits frequently interact only with the qubits next to them. So, some complex calculations are hard for superconducting circuits to perform effectively.

Ion Trap Quantum Computer

An atom in its neutral state has an equal number of protons (positively charged) and electrons (negatively charged). For example, a sodium atom in its neutral state has 11 protons and 11 electrons. But whenever the atom loses or gains an electron, it loses its neutral state and becomes either positively or negatively charged. Whenever an atom loses an electron, it becomes positively charged and called a *cation*. For example, if a sodium atom loses one electron, it becomes a sodium ion with a +1 charge. Whenever the atom gains an electron, it becomes negatively charged and called an *anion*. For example, a neutral chlorine atom has 17 electrons and 17 protons. When it gains one electron, it becomes a chlorine ion with a -1 charge. So, depending upon the electron gain and loss, an atom becomes an ion. That ion can be positively or negatively charged.

Each ion has an internal electronic state representing a quantum state. The ground state represents 0, and the excited state represents 1. They can be trapped and confined in free space with the help of electromagnetic fields. Quantum operations are performed by manipulating the states of ions using lasers or microwaves. Also, there is a possibility of entanglement because of ions' nature to interact with each other in controlled ways. This becomes critical for any quantum computing algorithms.

Advantages of Ion Trap Quantum Computer

These are the advantages:

- *Coherence* advantages *times*: Qubits in quantum computing must preserve their quantum state for as long as feasible to function properly. This is similar to trying to prevent a spinning top from tipping over. These "spinning tops" for ion trap quantum computers can maintain their upright position for a very long time, making them ideal for challenging tasks.

- *High accuracy*: A great degree of accuracy in calculations can be achieved by controlling the ions in an ion trap quantum computer with lasers.

- *Stronger interactions*: The ions, which serve as our qubits, are in close proximity and can easily interact with one another in ion trap quantum computers. Because qubits must interact to execute calculations, this is crucial for quantum computing. It feels like everyone can easily speak with one another in a tiny meeting area.

Demonstrations of Ion Trap Quantum Computer

In 2020, at NIST, a coherence time of up to 1 minute was achieved for beryllium ion qubits.

Ion trap qubits are said to achieve high fidelity. In recent years, several research groups have achieved 99 percent fidelity, which means only a 1 percent error rate occurs. Gate fidelity was said to be 99 percent to 99.1 percent, which means quantum gate operations are performed with less than 1 percent error rate.

Disadvantages of Ion Trap Quantum Computer

These are the disadvantages:

- *Sophisticated setups*: In ion trap quantum computers, precise control of individual ions requires sophisticated setups with manipulation of laser beams, radio frequency fields, and magnetic fields.

- *Communication between qubits*: Interactions between qubits are mediated with long-range Coulomb forces. The strength of interaction depends upon how close the qubits are. An increase in distance decreases the strength of interaction.

Topological Quantum Computer

You are probably familiar with the bits used by traditional computers, which can be either a 0 or a 1. These bits are the fundamental pieces of data needed to carry out any calculation, from launching a sophisticated machine learning model to merely loading a website.

Now, your business is interested in entering the quantum computing market. Qubits are a type of unit used in quantum computers in the place of bits. Qubits resemble enhanced bits. They can be both at the same time, according to the superposition principle of quantum physics, rather than merely being a 0 or a 1. Additionally, when two or more qubits are entangled, they can cooperate in ways that bits cannot, possibly enabling enormous improvements in processing power.

However, preserving the quantum state of qubits is a sensitive process, which makes quantum computing a significant difficulty. Errors can occur when these states are disrupted by noise or interference of any kind, including electromagnetic radiation and temperature variations. This is similar to what would happen if your old computer's bits randomly flip between 0 and 1. That would obviously be a serious issue!

Topological quantum computers designed with the goal of storing data in a way that makes it more reliable and resistant to errors brought on by outside influences. This is accomplished by the use of *anyons*, a specific type of particle that can exist in only two dimensions.

Imagine braiding together two strings that you have. Once braided, it makes little difference whether you move them around; they maintain their braided state. An essential concept behind a topological quantum computer is that. It is more resistant to "jostling" brought on by external conditions because the information is stored in the braiding of these anyons.

To put it briefly, the topological quantum computer was developed as a potential remedy for the issue of quantum error correction, which is one of the major challenges to the practical and scalable implementation of quantum computing. We might be able to more reliably perform quantum computations and get closer to the promise of quantum computing's incredible speed and power by improving the quantum state of qubits.

Advantages of Topological Quantum Computer

These are the advantages:

- *Error prone*: The main benefit of topological quantum computing is its resistance to errors, as was previously stated. Imagine that when you're editing a document, your computer makes a few unexpected word modifications. It would be highly frustrating and difficult to complete your assignment. The same is true with quantum computers; little adjustments or mistakes can cause serious issues. Topological quantum computers are less susceptible to these kinds of interruptions or "errors" due to the distinctive manner they store information (remember our braid analogy). This makes them more dependable.

- *Scalability*: It is extremely difficult to scale up and construct a big, functional quantum computer because qubits in conventional quantum computers must be carefully monitored and constantly adjusted to retain their quantum state. However, topological quantum computers might make it simpler to construct a large-scale quantum computer due to its error resistance. Consider it this way: managing a team is simpler when everyone is self-sufficient and doesn't need continual supervision.

- *Longer qubit states retention*: A significant obstacle in quantum computing is preserving qubits' quantum state across time. It's like attempting to maintain the exact equilibrium of a spinning top; ultimately, it wobbles and topples. The "braiding" of anyons in a topological quantum computer enables the system to maintain its quantum state for an extended period of time, offering a more stable foundation for challenging computations.

- *Secure*: The braiding of anyons serves as the storage medium for information in topological quantum computers. Now, to "read" the information covertly, someone would have to "unbraid" the anyons, which would inevitably leave traces. This makes these systems very safe and attractive in an era where cybersecurity is a key worry because it implies that any attempt to tamper with the information is detectable.

Disadvantages of Topological Quantum Computer

These are the disadvantages:

- *Technical complexity*: Non-Abelian anyons are a particular class of exotic particles necessary for topological quantum computers. These particles have not been physically detected, although they are being predicted by some condensed matter physics models. Significant problems exist in theoretical understanding and experimental implementation of finding and manipulating non-Abelian anyons.

- *Nonpractical application*: Topological quantum computing is based on an appealing but mostly unproven idea. Despite much theoretical effort, up until now research is going on to control anyons for computing or even establish with certainty that they exist.

- *Limited application*: Finally, the applicability of topological quantum computers may be rather constrained. With the "braiding" processes employed in topological quantum computing, several types of quantum algorithms could not be compatible. It's comparable to having a car that is really powerful but capable of traveling only on a certain sort of road; while fantastic on those routes, it is less useful elsewhere.

Photonic Quantum Computers

Photonic quantum computers use the property of photons. Here, photons act as qubits. According to the direction of photon travel, the photon can be either 0 or 1. But because of the superposition principle, the photon can be 0 and 1 simultaneously.

Purpose of Creating a Photonic Quantum Computer

These are some purposes:

- *Operational efficiency*: The cooling needed for conventional quantum computers, such as those built using superconducting circuits, is extremely high, usually near absolute zero. These regulations can dramatically increase operational expenses and create logistical difficulties. The ability of photonic quantum computers to function at room temperature may result in significant cost savings and improved usability.

- *High-speed processing*: In photonic quantum computers, photons, which act as the quantum bit (qubit), travel at the speed of light. This implies that computations might theoretically go extremely fast, providing real-time insights and quicker outcomes. With this speed, photonic quantum computing companies might have an advantage in highly competitive sectors.

- *Compatible infrastructure*: Photons are already used to carry information in many digital systems, particularly the Internet. For businesses that want to use photonic quantum computers, this interoperability with existing infrastructure could lower the cost of integration and adoption.

- *Scalability*: Given the widespread use and relatively simple synthesis and manipulation of photons, photonic quantum computers may be simpler to scale up. This implies that photonic quantum computers may be simpler and more affordable to upgrade as the need for more potent quantum computing increases. For potential future growth, this scalability may be a selling feature.

- *Market differentiation*: There is a potential for significant market differentiation because of the special advantages of photonic quantum computers. By providing a quantum computing solution that is possibly quicker, more scalable, and more effective, it may be possible to take a significant market share in the rapidly expanding quantum computing industry.

- *Fault tolerance*: Because of photons' noninteraction, photonic quantum computers have the potential for superior error correction and fault tolerance. This increased consistency can be a major selling advantage for companies that need accurate and consistent computations.

Advantages of Photonic Quantum Computer

Photonic quantum computers perform operations at room temperature, reducing the size of cooling systems.

Integrating existing fiber-optic-based telecommunications infrastructure helps connect quantum computers with networks and the quantum Internet.

Photons travel at the speed of light, which is the fastest possible speed in the universe. This might make photonic quantum computers extremely quick. Additionally, because photons hardly ever interact with one another, they don't readily lose energy to their environment. This might result in quantum computers using less energy.

Disadvantages of Photonic Quantum Computer

These are the disadvantages:

- *Technical complexity*: Although photons are excellent at moving fast and not interfering with one another, it is difficult to rely on them to properly transmit complex information.

- *Photon loss*: This is comparable to having a water hose leak while trying to water your yard. A portion of the water (or, in our instance, light) leaks out while traveling from point A to point B. This implies that some light does not reach its intended location, which may cause our calculations to be inaccurate.

- *Complex scaling*: Although we previously stated that photonic quantum computers may be more scalable, this does not imply that they are simple. It's comparable to having a chorus in which every photon is a member. Imagine managing a chorus of thousands or millions of singers. It's one thing to get a few choir members to sing in harmony. The more people there are, the more difficult it is to keep everyone on schedule and in tune.

- *High-quality setup*: For our system, we require specialized equipment: a dependable source to generate single photons and extremely accurate detectors to read them. It's comparable to attempting to play a vinyl record. A good record player serves as the source, and good speakers serve as the detectors. You won't be able to hear your music correctly if either of them isn't up to the task.

- *Early stages of development*: The field of photonic quantum computing is still developing. It's like if we have a working prototype for a novel new automobile, but we're still figuring out how to mass-produce it, ensure its reliability, and get it to function just as effectively in everyday situations as it does in the lab.

Note   The quantum computers discussed are in their developmental stage; the exact applications are not known at this time. Therefore, it's too early to compare each quantum computer with others.

Summary

This chapter discussed four prominent types of quantum computers in detail. Circuits used in superconducting quantum computers operate at extremely low temperatures and conduct electricity without resistance. These circuits, referred to as *qubits*, enable extraordinary processing capability since they can represent many states at once. They are based on quantum mechanical processes and have the ability to solve issues that classical machines are unable to. For topological quantum computers, by using "quasiparticles" that move in unique two-dimensional domains, topological quantum computers encode information. They base their calculations on "braiding" these particles, which is more error-proof than previous quantum systems' techniques. With this novel method, quantum computing should become more stable and reliable. For ion trap quantum computers, individual ions are maintained in place by electromagnetic fields and used as qubits. These ions are manipulated by lasers to carry out quantum operations. They offer a possible route for scalable quantum computation because of their potential for long coherence times and excellent precision. Photonic quantum computers using light particles (photons) as information carriers are capable of high-speed, naturally parallel processing. They carry out sophisticated calculations with less energy use with features such as entanglement and superposition. They provide a scalable, possibly more fault-tolerant method to quantum computing with their distinctive architecture.

CHAPTER 4

Assessing the Market and Competitive Landscape

In the ever-shifting landscape of business, the ability to assess and navigate the market is the foundation upon which successful ventures are built. This chapter is a crucial juncture in our journey toward unlocking the vast potential of quantum computing products and services. Here, we lay the groundwork for understanding the intricate web of opportunities, challenges, and dynamics that define the quantum computing market.

Introduction to Market Assessment

Before we delve into the world of market assessment, let's first understand what a market truly means. A market is where transactions take place, involving exchanges between various entities, be it individuals, organizations, governments, or businesses. These exchanges can involve goods, services, products, information, or anything else of value. In essence, a market is where demand and supply come together.

Take, for example, our everyday needs such as nutritious food, clothing, and housing. Each of these represents a form of demand. In response to these demands, numerous players or suppliers emerge, offering solutions to meet the varying desires, preferences, needs, and wants among us. This interaction creates a market. Similarly, consider the aviation industry; all airlines require planes for flying, leading to multiple players in the market providing such aircraft.

In this exchange, the supplier, who offers the service, product, or value, receives some form of reimbursement from those making the demand. This reimbursement may come in various forms, but it is a crucial aspect of the transaction.

D. Agarwal et al., *Productizing Quantum Computing*, https://doi.org/10.1007/978-1-4842-9985-2_4

Every business or organization today is built to address a specific problem or need, for which they receive reimbursement. Market assessment plays a vital role in understanding the type of problem that led to their existence and survival. There are various ways to conduct market assessment, but the fundamental principle remains the same: research for a market where there is sufficient untapped demand to sustain a business.

It's important to note that sustaining a business doesn't solely refer to making profits; it can also encompass reaching a break-even point, even for nonprofit organizations. The level of demand required to sustain a business varies based on the type of market. For instance, if you want to showcase your culinary skills by opening a restaurant, you'll aim to find just enough interested people so that you can cover the cost of your groceries, cooking utensils, time, transportation, and other expenses month over month.

Throughout this chapter, we will explore the top-down market assessment approach, which widely taught in various business schools worldwide. This approach provides valuable insights into understanding markets and identifying untapped opportunities.

By comprehending the principles of market assessment, we can lay a strong foundation for evaluating potential business opportunities and making informed decisions. So, let's embark on this journey of market assessment, unraveling the hidden potential of the markets we encounter.

Quantum Computing Market Landscape

Quantum computers are unlikely to become personal devices in the way that traditional computers ultimately became PC's and even tablets and smartphones.

As depicted in Figure 4-1, the quantum computing landscape is still in its nascent stages, with a significant emphasis on quantum computing hardware and manufacturing due to the complex challenges involved.

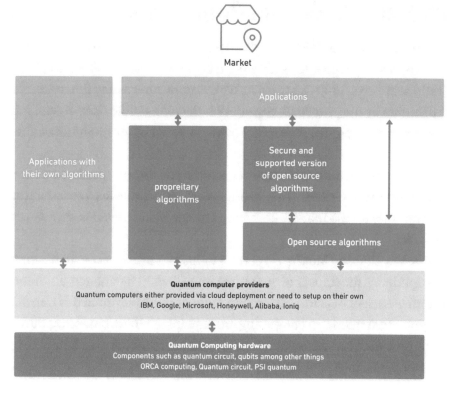

Figure 4-1. *High level overview of quantum platform*

Although there is ongoing research in both industry and academia concerning quantum algorithms, progress in this area is constrained by the current state of quantum computers they run on. Before providers can confidently claim to have a quantum computer that can function without errors, extensive research and development is required.

The focus on hardware is understandable because building stable and reliable quantum computers is no small feat. They are delicate systems that require precise control and isolation to maintain quantum coherence—the fragile state that enables quantum computation. Achieving error-free operation remains a significant hurdle. Classical everyday computers took 40 years to get created even if you start tracking development from 1940.

In summary, the quantum computing landscape is in a formative stage, with significant attention on hardware development. Advancements in quantum hardware will be crucial in unlocking the full potential of quantum algorithms, leading to the realization of powerful quantum computing capabilities in the future.

Market Size and Growth Projections

Based on industry reports published in this decade, the quantum computing market has already reached a significant size, estimated to be between $800 million to $1 billion. The projections are even more impressive, with experts forecasting the market to soar beyond $10 billion by the year 2030, considering the remarkable pace of scientific innovation. This demonstrates the rapid growth potential of the quantum computing landscape.

Across the quantum market, all industry reports consistently predict a minimum annual growth rate of 20 percent. This steady growth rate indicates a sustained and promising trajectory for the market, attracting attention from businesses, investors, and researchers alike.

According to a study by McKinsey, certain industries are expected to be among the first to experience the impact of quantum computing.[1] The finance, automotive, chemical, and life science sectors are among those at the forefront of this transformation. The developments in quantum computing are anticipated to revolutionize these industries by providing innovative solutions to complex problems and unlocking new possibilities for data analysis, simulations, and optimization.

As quantum computing technology continues to mature and become more accessible, its applications are expected to expand into other sectors, creating a wave of transformation and growth in various domains. This suggests that the quantum computing market's potential is not only significant today but will continue to evolve and flourish in the coming years, presenting abundant opportunities for businesses and entrepreneurs to explore and thrive in this promising landscape.

Key Players and Competitors in the Quantum Computing Market

As discussed in Chapter 4, the current focus of the tech industry is primarily on developing the necessary components for building an error-free quantum computer capable of running quantum algorithms. This pursuit has drawn the attention of universities, major tech companies, and startups, all dedicated to advancing quantum computing technology. Heavyweights such as Alibaba, Baidu, Nvidia, Amazon, Google,

---

[1] https://www.mckinsey.com/featured-insights/the-rise-of-quantum-computing

Intel, Microsoft, and IBM have made significant investments across various aspects of quantum computing, including chips, computers, simulation tools, language tools, and algorithms, all geared toward the goal of creating a robust quantum computing platform.

Telecommunication companies such as ATT, SK Telecom (South Korea), KPN (Netherlands), and British Telecom are also entering the quantum computing space to develop secure communication networks and improve Internet security. Startups like Alito Quantum and Arqit are actively working on quantum secure networks, contributing to the advancement of quantum technologies.

When it comes to application layers, the evolution appears reminiscent of the cloud computing market, with three key players.

- *Infrastructure as a service*: These providers offer software to monitor, manage, maintain, and create quantum computing platforms. Notable names in this category include 1Qbit, Agnostiq, and Entropica Labs.

- *Platform as a service*: These providers offer algorithms and tools for developers to build applications leveraging quantum computing platforms. This category also has multiple subclasses targeting niche segments such as data storage, processing and analysis, machine learning, artificial intelligence, robotics, simulation, and optimization, along with general service providers. Notable names in this category include AWS, IBM, Microsoft, D-Wave, Quantum Corporation, QCI, and Strangeworks.

- *Software as a service*: This category focuses on providing applications built on quantum computing platforms, allowing enterprises and consumers to achieve their desired outcomes. Notable players in this field include Algorithm IQ, HQS Quantum Simulations, Kuano, Proteinqure, Polaris QB, Quantum Generative Material, Multiverse Computing, and Star Quantum.

Currently, the quantum hardware, provider, and algorithm layers are experiencing significant activity and attention. In particular, cybersecurity in the algorithm layer is a top priority, as classical cryptography techniques are considered vulnerable.

The quantum computing landscape is evolving rapidly, driven by the combined efforts of industry leaders, researchers, and startups.

Market Segmentation

If you are an entrepreneur or corporate innovator interested in exploring the vast landscape of quantum computing, it is essential to start from a well-informed standpoint. Understanding the different segments (parts) of the market, including circuits, quantum computing platforms (hardware, tools, software), quantum algorithms, and applications, is crucial. Identifying where your strengths can be leveraged and weaknesses minimized is paramount before taking the plunge.

Strengths may take various forms, such as possessing strong domain expertise, abundant resources, capabilities in a niche field, valuable industry connections, substantial capital, efficient processes, or well-established distribution channels, among others. Conversely, these aspects may also reveal potential weaknesses. Therefore, a thoughtful analysis of the quantum market and a clear perception of your strengths and weaknesses will help you identify the most suitable market subsegment to enter.

Nevertheless, it is essential to be mindful of the decision-making process, as thorough research across users, customers, and the market will consume a significant amount of time. It is crucial to recognize that time, not money, is the most valuable resource for human beings.

For instance, let's consider a scenario where you possess a robust supply chain for raw materials, extensive fabrication design experience, and efficient manufacturing capabilities in producing classical components. In this case, becoming a supplier of quantum components, which can be integrated to build quantum circuits, presents a promising entry point into the market. However, before making a final decision, conducting comprehensive research is vital to ensure that this is indeed the best course of action for your business.

Why do you have more than a 0 chance of succeeding here? This is what is known as *competitive advantage* across the business literature.

You might be thinking that a lot of folks started with no strengths at all and yet succeeded; please think carefully. Apple had Steve Wozniak (expertise in making a functional computer) and Steve Jobs (making the functional computer friendly to use). Airbnb founders had a validated market and solution that nobody had. The Zoom founder via his previous stint with WebEx knew the customer needs and challenges that he could address.

Customers Job to Be Done

"Jobs to be done" was coined by Harvard business school professor Clayton Christensen as a way to understand why people buy certain products or services by identifying the specific problems they want to solve.

For example, in the case of Uber, the "job to be done" for customers is getting a convenient and reliable ride from one place to another without the hassle of driving or finding parking. Uber provides the solution with its user-friendly app and drivers to fulfill this need. Other alternatives to achieve this job include traditional taxis, public transport, rental cars, personal vehicles, walking, cycling, carpooling, and other ride-hailing apps.

In your chosen market segment, which is focused on quantum components, it is crucial to engage with the target personas who might have unsatisfied "jobs to be done." These target personas could include organizations, specific teams within those organizations, or even individual enthusiasts. For example, in the quantum component example, the target persona could be organizations or research institutions actively seeking to build quantum circuits.

By speaking directly with these target personas, you can understand their specific needs, pain points, and desires when it comes to quantum components. This will enable you to identify the exact problems they want to solve and the factors that matter most to them, such as performance, reliability, compatibility, or scalability.

To ascertain the necessary information for the quantum component market segment, engaging in conversations with potential customers and industry veterans is an effective method. There are more methods and techniques, but I find conversation to be most helpful. Here are the questions to explore during these conversations:

- What is the problem (job to be done) that people are hiring the product to fill or solve?

    a. What emotional factors drive their need for this solution?

    b. What social factors influence their decision to seek this product?

    c. What functional factors are crucial in fulfilling their requirements?

    d. How does the financial aspect play a role in their decision-making process?

    e.   Are there any potential life-saving applications for this product?

- What is the context or environment in which this specific problem arises?

  – Understanding the specific scenarios or use cases where the need for quantum components emerges.

- What are the barriers that are preventing them from accomplishing the job?

  – Identifying the challenges and obstacles that hinder customers from achieving their goals with current solutions.

- What do they feel when the job is accomplished?

  – Exploring the emotions and satisfaction levels when customers successfully address their needs using the quantum components.

- What other alternatives are they using to fill this job?

  a. Why do they hire or fire specific alternatives?

  – Understanding the factors influencing their choice of alternatives and what makes them switch between different solutions.

- What is the frequency of the job to be done?

  a. Is it an infrequent or frequent need?

  – Determining how often customers require quantum components to fulfill their specific needs.

- What is the urgency of the job to be done?

  a. Is the need for quantum components considered high, medium, or low priority?

  – Understanding the time sensitivity and importance of fulfilling the specific job.

- What is the motivation or core driving them to solve for it? Is it to save time or money? Is it to have meaning or showcase their authority? Or is it just curiosity?

  – Identifying the primary motivations behind their quest for quantum components, whether it's for practical reasons, personal growth, or curiosity-driven exploration.

- What is the trigger that makes them try to solve for this job to be done?

  – Exploring the events or circumstances that prompt customers to seek quantum components as a solution.

Engaging in numerous conversations with potential customers and industry veterans is a valuable approach to uncover patterns and commonalities across their needs and preferences. By actively listening to their feedback, you can identify a group of individuals or organizations expressing similar requirements and challenges. This shared sentiment among multiple stakeholders indicates the existence of distinct segments within the chosen market.

Mapping these segments based on the emerging patterns will provide a clearer understanding of the diverse target personas that make up the market. Each segment may have unique characteristics, preferences, and pain points.

Identifying Business Opportunities

Now we have understood how to identify a market segment and different target personas that exist inside that segment. It is important to understand which target persona to go after first and which ones to go after next. Take a look at Figure 4-2.

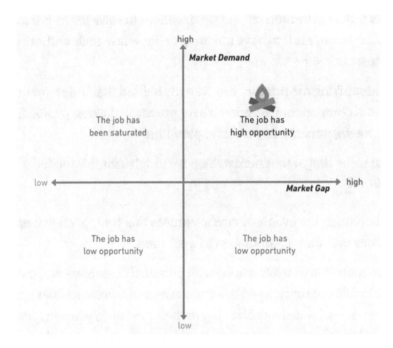

Figure 4-2. *2×2 quadrant for identifying market opportunities*

You can use this 2×2 matrix of market gap and market demand to plot different target jobs to be done (target personas). The upper-right quadrant is where the opportunity lies.

Summary

This chapter is a crucial guide for understanding the quantum computing market. It began by explaining the basics of markets and their importance. It then explored the early stages of quantum computing, emphasizing hardware development. The chapter also revealed the market's significant size and projected growth. It introduced key players and segments within the quantum computing market and explains the "jobs to be done" framework for understanding customer needs. Lastly, it discussed how to identify business opportunities by leveraging market gaps and competitive advantages. This chapter equipped you with the essential knowledge to navigate and capitalize on the quantum computing landscape.

CHAPTER 5

Designing Quantum Products and Services

This chapter is a comprehensive guide to designing quantum products and services that can help businesses effectively bring quantum technology to market.

In the previous chapter, we delved into the comprehensive process of analyzing the industry that caters to the market's needs. This exploration enabled us to identify a promising business opportunity within the market—one that remains underserved by the existing industry. A business opportunity is considered "viable" when customers are willing to pay for the solution and their payments exceed the costs involved in creating, marketing, and maintaining the product. This viability further allows for the establishment of a sustainable business model.

This process involves targeting an unmet need within a specific market segment and addressing it with a feasible workable solution. The term *feasible* in this context signifies the solution's technical achievability. Specifically, it relates to the potential to develop a product after a few years of research and development, contingent on the availability of adequate funding. For instance, endeavors like Neuralink's research into brain connectivity by Elon Musk or like Google's pursuit of a feasible quantum computer by companies are deemed feasible because of their financial capacity to support such long-term research and development endeavors.

However, your situation might vary. You could have an idea that is technically possible to execute today, eliminating the need for extensive research and development. On the other hand, your concept might require several years of research. In that case, it's essential to ascertain the required funding and evaluate whether you possess the necessary resources. The term *feasible* is subjective in this context, as it hinges on a variety of factors.

Remember, feasibility isn't solely about technical viability but also encompasses financial considerations, the potential for timely execution, and the alignment of your available resources with the project's requirements.

Defining Product Requirements

Continuing from our previous example, let's say you're developing quantum components for building quantum circuits and, subsequently, quantum computers. Through your research, both in the market and among customers, you've identified a specific need. Organizations, including big tech companies, startups, research institutions, and universities, require software to simulate interactions among quantum components. This software should facilitate testing, particularly when integrating third-party components with the ones you're producing.

You've gathered enough evidence to show that there's a demand in the market but not many solutions are available. You're eager to address this gap by creating a value proposition that meets this need.

It's advisable to document your findings, solution requirements, and how the market and customers will respond once your solution is launched and adopted. This documentation is often referred to as a *product requirements document* (PRD), a specification, a one-pager, or similar terms used in the product world. Jeff Bezos of Amazon introduced a concept called the *six-pager*, widely adopted in product development. You can easily find templates for this by searching online.

Irrespective of the name, the document's purpose is to crystallize your thinking and align your team on these key aspects:

- Identifying the customer's job to be done and its significance

- Defining the segment with the unfulfilled job

- Outlining the solution's functional and nonfunctional requirements

- Describing how the customer's experience will change after adopting the solution

- Establishing metrics to measure the solution's impact

- Discussing how the solution benefits your business in terms of retention, growth, and monetization

- Outlining your release strategy for bringing the solution to customers

As you've already grasped the first two points from previous chapters, I won't delve further into them.

When talking about solution requirements, we don't mean wireframes, prototypes, or the like. Instead, we're referring to the principles and criteria your solution must meet to be considered a viable answer to the customer's job to be done. These criteria can be divided into two types.

- *Functional*: Addressing the functional needs that must be fulfilled for customers to even consider adopting your solution. For instance, Facebook Messenger should allow users to send messages to friends.

- *Nonfunctional*: Addressing nonfunctional requirements that need to be met for customers to consider your solution. For instance, Facebook Messenger should be available 24/7, ensuring messages are promptly delivered.

You need to jot down both functional and nonfunctional criteria so that customers can even think about adopting your solution.

For our example of components and simulation software, it would look something like this:

Components

- Functional:

    a. Perform quantum operations near room temperature.

    b. Enable communication with various component types, including those from third parties.

- Nonfunctional:

    a. Achieve 100 percent reliability in performing operations.

    b. Complete each operation within a fraction of a second.

    c. Handle specific levels of current and wattage.

    d. Possess a defined shelf life.

    e. Maintain operational efficiency over a certain period.

Software

1. Functional:

    a. Support various operating systems and accessible through the Web.

    b. Compatibility with both third-party and in-house quantum components.

    c. Enable users to design, simulate, and analyze quantum circuits of varying complexity.

    d. Allow real-time collaboration and saving multiple designs.

    e. Provide prebuilt templates for user convenience.

2. Nonfunctional:

    a. Scalable to accommodate millions of users simultaneously.

    b. Operate around the clock, 365 days a year.

    c. Ensure fast loading and processing times.

    d. Achieve real-time collaboration in under a second.

    e. Guarantee data preservation without losses.

    f. Maintain enterprise-grade security.

Bear in mind that the given example aims to illustrate the concept. Actual requirements can be more detailed and incorporate additional factors. We can't confirm whether such a market exists and, if it does, what the customer's job and requirements entail.

Moving on, how will the customer's life look once they adopt the solution? This entails envisioning the customer's experience after they've adopted your solution. This is known as a *vision* in management terms, and it blends both science and art. You can creatively create an ambitious vision. For instance, Airbnb and Disney use storyboards to depict their visions. In your case, imagine that customer XYZ uses your software to design and simulate circuits before either ordering components through the software or requesting direct manufacturing and shipping. By doing so, XYZ reduces the time and costs involved in creating the circuit.

Using this vision, you can measure the solution's impact by comparing core benefits you offer against the customer's previous situation. This involves improving the time and cost efficiencies associated with circuit design. You can establish a baseline for these impact metrics using the current processes.

Regarding your business's perspective, you can discuss various aspects. Since businesses need to capture value to sustain and continually provide value to customers, it depends on your organization's goals. If you want to capture a market segment, you can measure the number of organizations using your software. If retaining customers and upselling components is a priority, consider organizations using your software and purchasing your components. If monetization is key, focus on the average revenue per organization you serve.

Lastly, discussing how you plan to release the solution to the market will be covered in other chapters of the book.

Introduction to Product Design

By now, you've documented everything you've learned about the market, the specific market segment, and the job that needs to be done within it. You've also laid out the criteria your solution should meet, as well as how you'll gauge its success from both customer and business perspectives.

Here, we're delving into the world of solution brainstorming. Think of brainstorming as a lively group activity where people gather to generate a variety of ideas for solving a problem. During this process, you and your team freely share thoughts without worrying about whether they're right or wrong. This atmosphere encourages creativity and sparks fresh, exciting solutions.

Various organizations and individuals have devised specific approaches to make brainstorming effective. The following are the main points to remember:

- You and your team should generate ideas aimed at solving the customer's job.

- Record these ideas without evaluating them initially.

- Use the solution criteria you've established to assess these ideas.

- Choose three to five ideas that seem promising and could be further evaluated with customers.

In our case, you need to do it twice for both the component and the service as that is our value proposition to solve customer jobs to be done in the target market segment.

After this initial brainstorming phase, it's time to create prototypes based on the selected ideas. These prototypes will be tested against the solution criteria you've set. If they meet these criteria, the next step involves engaging with customers to gather feedback. This feedback is crucial to validate whether you're addressing the right problem and whether your proposed solution is one that customers would be willing to pay for.

The entire process—starting with brainstorming, refining ideas, and moving on to prototype development—is collectively referred to as *product design*.

However, a key perspective should guide your product design journey. Keep the customer's job at the heart of your brainstorming sessions. When evaluating ideas, ensure they align with your solution criteria. When testing prototypes, seek feedback from customers to validate your solution's potential.

This approach, which centers on the customer's needs during brainstorming, evaluates ideas based on solution criteria, tests prototypes with customers, and embodies a customer-centric approach to product design. This approach significantly boosts the likelihood of creating a solution that truly resonates with your target audience.

Creating Product Prototypes

A prototype is like a model or a proof-of-concept version of something you want to create. It's not the final product, but it gives you a clear idea of what the real thing will be like. Just like how an artist might make a rough sketch before creating a detailed painting, a prototype helps you see how your idea will work and lets you test it to see if it's good before making the actual thing.

You have three to five ideas each for components and software. Now you will want to create the prototype for each of the ideas in a way that does not cost you a lot of money and time as well.

There are various ways to do it across software.

- *Paper prototyping*: Create hand-drawn sketches or paper-based interactive interfaces to visualize the flow and functionality of your software. It's a low-cost way to quickly iterate on design ideas.

- *Wireframing*: Using specialized software, design basic layouts and structures of your software's user interface. Wireframes focus on layout and navigation without including detailed visuals.

- *Mockups*: Develop more detailed visual representations of your software's interface, often including colors, fonts, and basic visuals. Mockups give stakeholders a better idea of the final look.

- *Interactive prototypes*: Using tools such as Adobe XD, Figma, or InVision, create clickable prototypes that allow users to interact with the software's interface as if it were real.

- *Wizard of Oz prototyping*: This technique involves simulating software functionality manually while users believe it's automated. This is useful for testing ideas before investing in full development.

The choice of technique depends on your project's stage, goals, and the level of interaction you want to simulate. Each technique offers specific benefits in terms of user feedback, functionality testing, and communication with stakeholders.

Similarly, there are various ways to do it for hardware. Here are some common methods:

- *Breadboarding*: This technique involves creating a circuit on a breadboard using discrete components, including transistors. It's a quick way to test transistor behavior and connections without soldering.

- *Circuit simulation software*: Using specialized software, you can simulate the behavior of transistor-based circuits. This allows you to test different configurations, voltages, and components virtually before building the physical prototype.

The choice of technique depends on the complexity of your transistor prototype, the desired level of fidelity, and your available resources. Each technique offers its own advantages in terms of speed, accuracy, and ease of experimentation.

Testing and Validating Prototypes with Customers

Now that you've generated various prototype ideas, the next step is to present these prototypes to the specific customers who have the corresponding "job to be done" that you're aiming to address. It is commonly also known as *alpha* or *beta* testing. In essence, you need to showcase the prototypes to your target audience.

The primary goal here is to confirm that at least one of the ideas, as represented by a prototype, meets the following criteria:

- *Desirability from a customer perspective*: Customers should express a genuine interest in hiring the solution to fulfill their "job to be done."

- *Viability for business sustainability*: Customers should demonstrate a willingness to pay for the solution, ensuring that your business can sustain itself while providing the solution.

- *Feasibility from a technical perspective*: The prototype should be technically feasible to be developed into a solution that can be offered to all customers.

Your interaction with customers involves showcasing the prototype and asking if they would consider hiring it to fulfill their needs. If they show interest, you'd delve deeper into understanding their motivations and ideally gather a commitment from them. This commitment might come in the form of their time, money, or referrals to bring in more customers. If they're not interested, you want to understand the reasons behind their decision.

This approach is commonly referred to as *lean testing*, a concept popularized by Eric Ries in his book *The Lean Startup*. The idea is to test your concepts while minimizing the investment of effort, time, and money. The goal is to determine if your idea can effectively address the customer's "job to be done," create a viable business, and assess its feasibility. This lean approach focuses on testing desirability, viability, and feasibility without overextending resources in terms of effort, money, and time.

Now, you might end up with a prototype (or an idea) that customers find desirable, viable, and feasible, or you might not. If you do have a promising concept, proceed to transform the prototype into a fully-fledged user experience, establish a business, and release the experience to the customer. However, if you don't meet the criteria, you'll need to revisit either the target segment, the job to be done, the idea, or all of them. Remember, this is an iterative process, not a linear one.

User Experience Design

User experience (UX) encompasses how individuals feel and engage with products, services, or systems. It's the overall impression during use, whether of a website, app, gadget, or physical space.

Think of it like visiting a new restaurant. The food, ambiance, and service shape your experience. Similarly, websites or apps involve design, ease of finding what you need, and smooth functionality—all contributing to your user experience.

Good UX ensures enjoyment, efficiency, and logical use. It reflects the creator's understanding your needs, providing a seamless and positive experience. Conversely, bad UX can lead to frustration, confusion, and annoyance.

In essence, user experience revolves around emotions and functionality. It prioritizes making tasks easy, enjoyable, and effective for users.

Once you have a prototype that's desirable, viable, and feasible, it's time to convert it into a comprehensive user experience. This experience encompasses the entire user journey, from awareness of the solution to hiring it and accomplishing the task.

Several resources delve into achieving great user experience, but I'll summarize with five key principles.

- *User-centered*: Prioritize user needs and preferences. For instance, when designing a banking app, conduct research to understand specific requirements such as quick balance checks and secure logins.

- *Simplicity*: Keep designs straightforward for easy understanding. In a fitness tracking app, emphasize core features such as steps, calories, and goals rather than overwhelming users with complex menus.

- *Consistency*: Maintain uniform design elements for a cohesive experience. Whether in website colors or font styles, consistency helps users navigate seamlessly.

- *Feedback*: Offer immediate responses to user actions for clarity. An e-commerce app confirming an item's addition to the cart reassures users, creating a clear feedback loop.

- *Testing and iteration*: Continuously enhance through user testing and design refinement. Regularly gathering feedback and adjusting layouts based on user responses ensures an intuitive experience.

In sum, by prioritizing emotions and functionality, UX ensures users find tasks enjoyable, efficient, and effective. We need to convert our prototype (and idea) into an experience using these principles.

Hardware and Software Integration

Hardware and software integration means making physical parts (hardware) work smoothly with programs (software) in a device. Firmware is also involved as it is merely software, and for the sake of simplicity, we are covering it along with software. When integrated well, they create a seamless user experience. This ensures hardware supports software's functions and software utilizes hardware's abilities.

For instance, in a smartphone, hardware and software integration makes components such as the display, camera, and processor work together with apps and the operating system. This gives us features such as touch control, good photos, and smooth multitasking.

In our case with quantum components and simulation software, extensive integration might not be needed. But for something like offering a quantum computer as a service, these five principles help:

- *Smooth interaction*: Ensure hardware and software work well together, like smart home devices connecting through an app.

- *User-focused design*: Put user needs first in both hardware and software, such as a fitness tracker syncing data with a simple app.

- *Consistent experience*: Keep the same look and feel across hardware and software, like a car's system matching its app.

- *Strong security*: Protect data in both hardware and software, like using biometrics to unlock a smartphone and apps.

- *Optimized performance*: Make both parts work efficiently, such as GPUs designed for smooth gaming with gaming software.

Challenges of Designing Quantum Products and Services

Developing a quantum product, service, or solution, or a hybrid of these, can present a range of challenges. The top 10 challenges you might encounter are as follows. The extent to which you face these challenges will depend on the nature of the solution you're working on.

- *Limited use cases*: Quantum technology's practical applications are still emerging, posing a challenge in identifying viable use cases. Companies must strike a balance between research and development while seeking market-fit solutions. Engaging with various industries and academic institutions can help explore diverse quantum technology applications. Foster partnerships with organizations that can benefit from quantum solutions in areas such as cryptography, optimization, and material science.

- *Error correction*: Quantum systems are susceptible to errors due to environmental factors and quantum decoherence (*Quantum decoherence* is when the fragile quantum properties of particles, like superposition and entanglement, break down and become regular, classical properties due to interactions with their environment. It's like a delicate soap bubble popping when it touches something, causing the quantum state to collapse into a more predictable classical state.) Establishing effective error correction methods is pivotal for ensuring reliable quantum computing. Research and develop robust error correction codes and fault-tolerant techniques. Prioritize enhancing qubit coherence times and investigating strategies for error mitigation.

- *Interoperability*: The presence of different quantum hardware platforms and programming languages poses a challenge in creating universally compatible quantum solutions. Achieving interoperability across diverse quantum technologies is essential for broader adoption. Advocating for standardized programming languages and hardware interfaces is crucial. Collaboration with quantum hardware manufacturers is needed to establish common protocols for seamless integration.

- *Technical complexity*: Quantum technology is characterized by high complexity, demanding specialized knowledge in quantum mechanics and advanced engineering. Developing and maintaining quantum hardware and software requires expertise that is relatively limited. Investment in specialized training and education for employees can bridge the knowledge gap. Encouraging collaborations among physicists, researchers, and engineers can help address technical challenges effectively.

- *Talent shortage*: The quantum technology field faces a shortage of skilled professionals, spanning from physicists to software engineers. Building a skilled workforce proficient in quantum technology remains an ongoing challenge. Partnering with universities to offer specialized courses in quantum technology and creating internship programs can attract and nurture young talent in the field.

- *Cost*: Quantum hardware and development entail substantial expenses because of the need for specialized equipment and expertise. Overcoming cost barriers to make quantum solutions accessible is a significant challenge. Exploring cost-sharing models through partnerships and consortiums can alleviate financial constraints. Focusing on optimizing manufacturing processes is essential for reducing production costs.

- *Resource intensive*: Quantum systems often demand extreme cooling and isolation for optimal operation. The infrastructure requirements for quantum technology can be both expensive and energy-intensive. Exploring energy-efficient cooling solutions and environmentally friendly technologies for quantum hardware is essential. Collaboration with experts in energy management can lead to optimized resource utilization.

- *Scalability*: Scaling up quantum systems while maintaining coherence is a complex task. Increasing qubit count while preserving stability poses a significant challenge. Investment in research to overcome scalability limitations through techniques like error-corrected qubits and topological qubits is crucial. Collaborating with experts in materials science and fabrication can contribute to improving qubit stability.

- *Education and awareness*: Educating the public, potential customers, and decision-makers about the benefits and limitations of quantum technology is vital. Raising awareness and enhancing understanding can significantly impact adoption rates. Organizing workshops, seminars, and public talks to educate a broader audience about quantum technology is essential. Collaborating with educational institutions to develop educational materials for students and professionals can contribute to building knowledge.

- *Regulation and standards*: As quantum technology evolves, regulatory frameworks and industry standards are still evolving. Navigating the legal and compliance aspects can be intricate. Collaborating with legal experts and policymakers to shape regulations that encourage innovation while ensuring the safety and ethical use of quantum technology is important. Active participation in industry associations and standards bodies can contribute to the development of best practices.

Addressing these challenges requires collaborative efforts among researchers, industry players, governments, and educational institutions. This collaboration fosters innovation, research, and the practical implementation of quantum products, services, and solutions.

While these challenges might seem daunting, the examples shared earlier and our analysis of the market landscape demonstrate that numerous companies, research organizations, startups, and universities are investing in the quantum space with significant venture capital. A potential market exists here, and those who have invested stand to reap substantial rewards when this market fully materializes. The potential for a vast and untapped market, coupled with new problem-solving opportunities, underscores the value of this innovative domain.

Security and Privacy Considerations

Developing quantum products, services, solutions, or hybrids involves various legal, privacy, compliance, and security considerations. As quantum technologies advance, these aspects become increasingly important. Here are some key areas to consider, along with relevant examples of current laws:

- *Intellectual property protection*: Patents and intellectual property rights are crucial for safeguarding quantum innovations. For example, the U.S. Patent and Trademark Office (USPTO) grants patents for quantum-related inventions, such as quantum computing algorithms or quantum cryptography methods.

- *Data privacy and security*: Quantum technologies can have implications for data security and privacy. For example, the General Data Protection Regulation (GDPR) in the European Union imposes strict requirements on handling personal data, regardless of the technology used. Quantum systems that process personal data must comply with GDPR.

- *Export controls*: Quantum technologies may fall under export control regulations because of potential dual-use applications. For example, the Wassenaar Arrangement lists certain dual-use items subject to export controls, including technologies related to cryptography, which quantum encryption falls under.

- *Cybersecurity and cryptography*: Quantum computing could impact classical encryption methods, requiring updates in cryptography standards. For example, the National Institute of Standards and Technology (NIST) is working on post-quantum cryptography standards to address the potential threat quantum computers pose to classical encryption.

- *Ethical considerations*: The ethical use of quantum technologies must be considered, including potential risks and benefits. For example, ethical guidelines for research involving quantum technologies are outlined by various institutions and organizations to ensure responsible development. We have similar considerations in AI called responsible AI.

- *Data handling and processing*: Quantum computing's unique capabilities could raise questions about data handling and processing practices. For example, laws like the California Consumer Privacy Act (CCPA) in the United States set requirements for handling consumer data, including data collected by quantum systems.

- *Standards and regulations*: As quantum technologies become more prevalent, standards and regulations specific to quantum could emerge. The U.S. National Quantum Initiative Act supports quantum research and establishes a program to encourage standards development and coordination.

- *Health and safety*: Quantum technologies involving hardware could have health and safety considerations. For example, regulations like the Occupational Safety and Health Administration (OSHA) guidelines in the United States could apply to workplaces involving quantum hardware.

- *International collaboration*: Global collaboration in quantum research requires adherence to international norms and laws. For example, international treaties and agreements, such as the Wassenaar Arrangement, address the export of certain dual-use technologies, including those related to quantum.

- *Liability and regulation gaps*: As quantum technologies evolve, liability and regulatory gaps might emerge. For example, legal frameworks may need to adapt to address scenarios where quantum technologies result in unintended consequences or security breaches.

It's important to note that as quantum technologies continue to develop, legal and regulatory landscapes may evolve accordingly. Staying informed about relevant laws, collaborating with legal experts, and proactively addressing legal, privacy, compliance, and security concerns are essential for responsible and successful development in the quantum space.

Collaborating in Cross-Functional Teams

A cross-functional team is like a team of superheroes with different powers teaming up to solve a giant puzzle. Each person has their own unique ability—one might be great at drawing, another at crunching numbers, and someone else might know a ton about computers. When they work together, they finish the puzzle quicker and better than if they were working alone. It's like putting together a jigsaw puzzle where everyone's skills fit together perfectly.

When it comes to building products, a variety of people with different skills are needed. At a minimum, you'll require a designer, product manager, engineer, and data analyst. Sometimes you might need a marketer and researcher, and in more complex cases, like with quantum services or solutions, even more experts like researchers and physicists might be essential.

To make sure your cross-functional team works well together, follow these five principles that have proven to set teams up for success:

- *Collaborate openly*: Communication is key. Share information and work together toward a common goal. For example, if engineers are building a software feature while designers are crafting the user interface, regular meetings between these teams ensure everyone understands the technical needs and design requirements. This leads to a cohesive final product.

- *Value expertise*: Every team member brings a unique set of skills. Recognizing and appreciating each person's contribution forms a strong foundation for collaboration. In a marketing campaign, content writers, graphic designers, and data analysts each play a crucial role. By respecting these diverse skills, the team creates a comprehensive campaign that resonates with the target audience.

- *Decide together*: Decisions should involve input from all relevant team members. Different perspectives enrich the decision-making process, resulting in well-rounded choices. When deciding on a project timeline, involving representatives from development, design, and marketing ensures a feasible timeline that aligns with everyone's responsibilities.

- *Adapt and solve*: Unexpected challenges often arise, requiring creative problem-solving. Being adaptable and open to new approaches helps the team overcome obstacles effectively. For instance, a product development team might face a sudden change in requirements due to customer feedback. Collaborative brainstorming allows them to adapt quickly while staying on course.

- *Trust and empower*: Empower team members to make decisions within their expertise. Trusting each other's capabilities fosters ownership and accountability. In a cross-functional team working on a sales strategy, the leader empowers members to handle specific parts. This trust boosts motivation and allows each person to contribute effectively.

Remember, these principles are the building blocks of successful cross-functional collaboration. By following them, you'll enhance teamwork and achieve better outcomes. Just like superheroes combining their strengths, your team can create something incredible by working together!

The Role of Product Managers Throughout the Process

A product manager (PM) is a central figure in the entire life cycle of a product, service, solution, or hybrid. Serving as the bridge between different teams, the PM ensures seamless collaboration to create a quantum offering that aligns with customer demands, business objectives, and technical feasibility.

During the brainstorming phase, the product manager initiates collaborative sessions involving physicists, engineers, software developers, and researchers. By amalgamating insights on quantum advancements, market trends, and strategic goals, the PM sets the foundation for a groundbreaking quantum solution. For instance, consider the development of a quantum computing service that aims to solve complex optimization problems for industries.

As the ideation narrows down and prototyping takes shape, the product manager guides the process, considering technical viability, user value, and alignment with the company's vision. In the quantum computing example, the PM may prioritize a prototype that enables users to submit optimization tasks and receive quantum-assisted solutions. This requires close coordination with quantum physicists and software engineers to actualize the solution's functionality.

In the prototype testing phase, the product manager takes on the role of a feedback collector. By organizing test sessions with potential users, the PM gathers insights into the prototype's performance and usability. In the quantum computing context, the PM might identify challenges users face while interacting with the quantum interface, which informs iterative improvements.

In scenarios involving hardware and software integration for quantum solutions, the product manager orchestrates the synergy between the two domains. In the quantum computing project, this could involve integrating quantum processors with software platforms. The PM facilitates communication between quantum hardware teams and software developers to ensure a seamless experience for users.

Effective cross-functional teamwork is the forte of the product manager. They ensure all teams comprehend the quantum solution's technicalities, user requirements, and market positioning. Regular meetings aid in conveying quantum concepts to developers and designers, ensuring a cohesive and user-friendly quantum experience.

Moreover, the product manager shoulders the responsibility of addressing legal, security, and compliance aspects in the quantum domain. Collaborating with legal experts, the PM ensures that quantum data handling adheres to relevant regulations. Working with cybersecurity professionals, they implement encryption and authentication measures to safeguard sensitive quantum information.

Finally, releasing the quantum solution is a meticulously orchestrated endeavor guided by the PM. Collaborating with marketing teams, the PM devises a comprehensive launch strategy that includes awareness campaigns, industry conferences, and targeted outreach to quantum enthusiasts. Post-launch, the PM oversees user feedback collection and monitors key performance indicators to identify areas for enhancement.

In essence, the product manager plays a pivotal role in driving the success of a quantum product, service, solution, or hybrid. By fostering collaboration, navigating intricate technicalities, and ensuring compliance, the PM helps deliver a quantum innovation that transforms industries and addresses complex challenges.

Summary

This chapter discussed designing quantum products and services. The goal was to guide you in bringing quantum technology to the market effectively. It started with defining the requirements for the product and then introduces the basics of product design. Next, it discussed the creation of product prototypes and emphasized the importance of testing and validating these prototypes with customers. User experience design is also highlighted as a crucial aspect. The chapter acknowledges the challenges in designing quantum products and services and addresses security and privacy considerations. It emphasized collaboration in cross-functional teams and underscored the role of product managers through all of it.

CHAPTER 6

Developing a Quantum Roadmap

In the world of quantum development, creating a roadmap is akin to plotting a course through uncharted territory. This chapter is your guide to this crucial process, beginning with an introduction to product roadmaps and objectives and key results (OKRs). We'll delve into the nitty-gritty of defining objectives and identifying key results along with helping you estimate resource requirements and timelines accurately. To ensure your quantum journey stays on track, we'll also explore risk assessment and mitigation strategies. You'll gain insights into the most common risks in quantum development, discover how to structure your outcomes effectively, and master the art of communication and stakeholder management. Finally, we'll show you how to measure progress and, if necessary, adjust your roadmap to navigate the ever-evolving quantum landscape.

Introduction to Product Roadmaps

To start, it's crucial to understand what a product roadmap is all about and why it matters.

Imagine you're gearing up for an exciting road trip to a special destination. To ensure a smooth journey, you sketch out a map that highlights where you're beginning, the significant places you'll stop, the choices you'll make, and the steps necessary to reach your destination.

In the realm of product development, think of a product roadmap as your guiding map. It directs your path while you embark on the adventure of creating a new product or enhancing an existing one. Just as a travel map helps you decide where to pause for food, rest, and captivating sights along the way, a product roadmap aids your team in choosing which features to create, when to develop them, and how they all fit together.

© Dhairyya Agarwal, Shalini D and Srinjoy Ganguly 2023
D. Agarwal et al., *Productizing Quantum Computing*, https://doi.org/10.1007/978-1-4842-9985-2_6

It establishes a timeline, goals, and priorities for the product's growth. And much like adapting travel plans because of unforeseen circumstances, a product roadmap can be adjusted as your team learns and adapts.

In simple terms, a product roadmap is your tailored travel itinerary for crafting a product. It charts the journey from start to finish, ensuring your team stays organized and on track.

You'll discover that the product requirement document or the solution you devised in Chapter 5 can be skillfully transformed into a roadmap. Even the enhancements for that solution can be laid out using a roadmap approach.

Now, you might be curious about where this journey begins and where it leads.

Introduction to Objectives and Key Results

Think of the starting point on the roadmap as the current state of your customer's needs. The destination represents the future state once you've successfully met those needs. This is likely described in your product requirement document or mission statement.

Just as you track your progress on a road trip by measuring the distance traveled, you also need a way to measure your progress in solving your customer's needs and moving toward your destination. Remember, this concept was discussed in the product requirements document as part of "establishing metrics to measure the solution's impact."

You can measure progress in two fundamental ways.

- *Customer impact*: How effectively does your solution meet the customers' needs compared to alternatives?

- *Business impact*: How does your business benefit by addressing the customers' needs?

In the world of tech management, these measurements are known as *objectives and key results*.

- *Objective*: Think of the objective as the ultimate goal of your journey. It's similar to saying, "I want to have an incredible adventure and create unforgettable memories on this trip." This overarching goal guides your actions. Consider a company that designs bicycles. Their objective might be "Becoming a top choice for eco-friendly transportation."

- *Key results*: Key results act like markers along the way, indicating progress toward your objective. They are specific and measurable. For instance, for the bicycle company, key results could include "Increase sales by 20% this quarter" and "Achieve 90% positive customer feedback regarding our eco-friendly initiatives."

This approach takes into account both the impact on customers and the impact on the business. Positive feedback reflects the fulfillment of customer needs, while increased sales capture the business value from meeting those needs.

In simpler terms, the objective is your main purpose, and the key results are the concrete actions you'll take to ensure you're reaching your goal.

By defining these objectives and key results, your company gains clear direction. Measuring progress against these milestones ensures you're moving in the right direction. Much like a road trip, the objective sets the destination, and the key results act as planned stops, making sure you're on course and achieving your intended outcomes.

Now you might be wondering how to apply this concept to the quantum computing business, the hypothetical example we've been discussing so far.

Defining the Objective and Key Results

Defining OKRs is akin to setting a substantial goal and breaking it down into specific steps to achieve that goal. It's a way to ensure you're headed in the right direction and making substantial progress. Let's simplify the process with straightforward steps and best practices:

Step 1: Define Your Objective

- Begin by contemplating your main goal, or your genuine aspiration. This is comparable to saying, "I aspire to create exceptional quantum components to accelerate the advancement of quantum computing."

Step 2: Make It Specific

- While your objective represents the overarching vision, now it's time to add precision. For instance, in the context of quantum components, your objective could evolve into "Emerge as the acknowledged industry standard for quantum components and simulation software."

Step 3: Set Measurable and Realistic Key Results

– Picture key results as miniature goals or markers showcasing your proximity to the primary objective. These markers are akin to milestones on your journey. They must be easily quantifiable and evidence that genuine progress is unfolding. The markers should challenge you yet remain attainable within your resources and capabilities. Importantly, they should be rooted in actual customer benefits.

– For the quantum computing example, conceivable key results might include the following:

  – "At least 80% of companies using our solution adopt it at least once a month for a year."

  – "At least 40% of companies ordering and utilizing our chips continue placing orders every quarter."

  – "More than 100 companies are proactively utilizing our simulation solution by the conclusion of the first year."

  – "We have secured orders from more than 20 companies for our components by the culmination of the first year."

Step 4: Connect Key Results to Your Objective

– Your key results should serve as direct contributors to your primary objective. Visualize them as the steps that propel you toward your ambitious goal. In the analogy of the bicycle company, augmenting sales and garnering favorable customer feedback are pivotal strides toward becoming a premier choice for environmentally friendly transportation.

The following are best practices:

– Maintain simplicity and clarity. The entire team should comprehend the objective and key results.

– Concentrate on a select number of key results. An excess can lead to overwhelming complexity.

- Embrace adaptability. If something isn't going according to plan, you can recalibrate your key results—akin to altering your travel itinerary when faced with unforeseen roadblocks.

- Engage your entire team. Every team member should be familiar with the objective and key results, and they can contribute insights on how to attain them.

Consider OKRs as your roadmap to triumph. Your objective mirrors the destination you're striving for, and the key results stand as pivotal milestones on the journey, substantiating your progress toward the ultimate goal. Comparable to a road trip's need for milestones to remain on course, your OKRs ensure you're perpetually advancing on the path to success.

Now, you might be pondering where the actual efforts to progress on the key results toward reaching the objective lie and how they are structured within a roadmap.

Identifying Key Deliverables

Now, this is where things can become a bit intricate. While the term *deliverables* might make you think of documents like the product requirement document, validated solution prototypes, hardware components, or software mockups, we're actually discussing deliverables for your customers in this context.

But it's not about just one individual customer; we're talking about a group of customers.

A deliverable is something you provide to customers who have a specific job to be done. This deliverable serves to progress your key result or signal that you're moving in the right direction to achieve that key result.

These deliverables can originate from various sources, such as the following:

- Insights gained from market and customer research as explored in Chapter 4

- New technological capabilities developed by your technical team

- Direct customer feedback

- Data analytics

- – Brainstorming sessions focused on the user journey and the job to be done

- – The company's vision and areas where improvements are needed

- – And many other places.

For our hypothetical quantum components example, you might have a single deliverable based on the fictional product requirement document discussed in Chapter 5. However, depending on the available development resources, based on your funding, you could also have multiple product requirement documents, each outlining a unique aspect. For example, see the following table:

Objective	Customer Key Result	Business Key Result	Deliverables
Emerge as the acknowledged industry standard for quantum components and simulation software	"At least 80% of companies using our solution adopt it at least once a month for a year."	"More than 100 companies are proactively utilizing our simulation solution by the conclusion of the first year."	Initiative 1: Simulation software. Initiative 3: Integrated buying experience from software.
	"At least 40% of companies ordering and utilizing our chips continue placing orders every quarter."	"We have secured orders from more than 20 companies for our components by the culmination of the first year."	Initiative 2: Quantum components. Initiative 4: Components and software integration.

Here are the deliverables:

- *Initiative 1*: Simulation software

- *Initiative 2*: Quantum components

- *Initiative 3*: Integrated buying experience from software

- *Initiative 4*: Components and software integration

Estimating Resource Requirements and the Timeline

Estimating resource requirements and timelines is a pivotal step in the roadmap creation process. Once you have a comprehensive understanding of your various product initiatives and their scopes, the task at hand is to determine the necessary time, resources, and costs needed to bring these endeavors to fruition. This phase involves breaking down each deliverable into specific tasks, estimating the effort required for each task, and subsequently allocating costs. The collective sum of these estimates lays the groundwork for establishing the required resources and the timeline for your projects.

The estimation process differs for hardware and software initiatives because of their unique characteristics:

- *Hardware projects*: These often entail physical components and intricate manufacturing processes.

    - Estimating hardware projects can be intricate due to dependencies on suppliers, manufacturing lead times, and potential delays.

    - Aspects such as component sourcing, assembly, testing, and quality control must be carefully considered.

    - Prototyping and testing iterations hold immense importance and can influence both the timeline and budget.

- *Software projects*: Agile methodologies empower software projects to undergo incremental development, enabling adjustments based on user feedback.

For accurate estimation, it is vital to involve domain experts in both scenarios. Let's consider an example of working on multiple customer deliverables within the hypothetical quantum circuit context:

Initiative 1, Simulation software: Engage software developers.

Initiative 2, Quantum components: Involve hardware developers, quantum researchers, and physicists.

Initiative 3, Integrated buying experience: Collaborate with software developers and network engineers.

Initiative 4, Components and software integration: Engage firmware engineers, software engineers, and hardware developers.

Experts from each domain have provided these insights:

- **Initiative 1: Simulation software**

  - Resources: Four software engineers

  - Dependency: None

  - Timeline: Six months for development (90 percent accurate)

  - Phases: Can be shipped weekly, monthly, or quarterly.

- **Initiative 2: Quantum components**

  - Resources: Four researchers, two physicists, two hardware engineers

  - Dependency: Yes

  - Timeline: Eight months for research, four months for shipping (80 percent accurate)

  - Phases: Can be shipped only at the end of 12 months

- **Initiative 3: Integrated buying experience**

  - Resources: Two software engineers, one network engineer

  - Dependency: On initiative 1

  - Timeline: Two weeks for research, two months for development (70 percent accurate)

  - Phases: Can be shipped weekly, monthly, or quarterly

- **Initiative 4: Components and software integration**

  - Resources: One software engineer, two firmware engineers, one hardware engineer

  - Dependency: On initiatives 1 and 2

- Timeline: Two months for research, two months for development (50 percent accurate)

- Phases: Can be shipped at the end of four months

With the cost estimates in hand, your next step involves deciding the scope of each initiative based on available funding. Whether you operate within a large corporation or receive funding from venture capitalists, friends and family, or financial institutions, these estimates guide your decisions. For instance, in the quantum component example, you might choose to fund the first three initiatives as follows:

- Initiatives 1 and 2 run in parallel.

- Initiative 3 begins after initiative 1 is completed.

Alternatively, because of the specialized expertise required for initiative 2, you might opt to fund only initiatives 1 and 3.

Assessing Risks and Mitigations

Imagine you're planning a big outdoor picnic. You know that the weather can be unpredictable and there's a chance it might rain. So, what do you do? You might bring an umbrella, just in case, or choose a backup indoor location. This is a bit like risk management!

Risk management is all about thinking ahead and getting ready for things that might not go as planned. It means spotting possible problems or "risks" that could happen and finding ways to deal with them. This is important because it helps you be prepared for surprises and avoid unexpected troubles.

In our everyday life, we use risk management without even realizing it. For example, wearing a helmet while riding a bike is a way to manage the risk of getting hurt. In business or projects, like creating a new product, risk management helps prevent problems from ruining the plan. It's like having a backup plan in case things don't go smoothly.

So, just like packing an umbrella for a picnic, risk management is about being ready for challenges, so you can enjoy your picnic or smoothly achieve your objectives as a product manager.

For any product initiative, you can follow these steps to identify risks and come up with plans to manage them:

- *Identify risks*: Think about things that could cause issues or delays.

- *Consider impact*: Understand how bad each risk could be if it happens.

- *Estimate likelihood*: Think about how likely each risk is to actually occur.

- *Plan prevention*: Find ways to stop risks from happening or reduce their impact.

- *Have backup plans*: Be ready with a plan if a risk happens despite your efforts.

- *Get expert help*: Talk to people who know about different areas to spot risks you might miss.

- *Check regularly*: Keep looking for new risks or changes in existing ones.

- *Stay flexible*: Be prepared to deal with challenges, even if you can't avoid every risk.

By doing these steps, you'll be well-prepared for anything that might come your way during your project.

Most Common Risks in Quantum Development

Here are five important risks to consider when investing in quantum development:

- *Lack of expertise*:

  - *Risk*: Quantum development needs specialized knowledge, and there might not be enough skilled professionals.

  - *Solution*: Train your team and partner with experts from research institutions or consultants.

- *Rapidly changing field*:
  - *Risk*: Quantum technology evolves quickly, and it's tough to keep up.
  - *Solution*: Keep learning, attend events, and collaborate to stay updated.
- *Unpredictable hardware performance*:
  - *Risk*: Quantum hardware can be unpredictable because of errors and instability.
  - *Solution*: Develop error-correcting methods and test algorithms thoroughly.
- *Limited quantum resources*:
  - *Risk*: Access to quantum computing resources can be limited.
  - *Solution*: Use cloud-based platforms and hybrid algorithms to maximize resources.
- *Complex algorithm design*:
  - *Risk*: Developing quantum algorithms is tricky and mistakes can lead to inefficiencies.
  - *Solution*: Work with experts, start with simpler problems, and test on simulations.

Remember, addressing these risks helps quantum development become more reliable and contributes to advancements in the field. Also, consider protecting your innovative solutions through intellectual property safeguards such as patents and copyrights. Consulting legal experts can be helpful for this aspect.

Structuring the Outcomes

You might come across the term *prioritization* frequently when discussing roadmaps. Prioritization involves deciding which deliverables to focus on based on factors such as the market, the customer needs, and the current state of the business. From my perspective, prioritization is deciding on business objectives and key results. Once you have that alignment, you can then prioritize deliverables based on considerations such as funding, cost, risk, and dependencies.

We've previously established a hypothetical prioritized roadmap for quantum components, taking into account funding, cost, risk, and dependencies.

Now that you understand the objective, key results, deliverables, budgeting, and risk management, you can bring everything together into a structured product roadmap. This roadmap outlines when each deliverable will be delivered in a way that drives the key results and objective.

This approach is one we follow, as it connects the "why" (objective) with the "what" (key result) and then further connects the "how" and "when" (deliverables and timeline). Consider the following structure:

Objective	Customer Key Result	Business Key Result	Time Period 1	Time Period 2 ..	Time Period n
Objective 1	Key result 1	Key result 2	Deliverable "a"	Deliverable "d"	Deliverable "aa"
	Key result 3	Key result 4	Deliverable "b"	Deliverable "e"	Deliverable bb"
Objective 2	Key result 5	Key result 6	Deliverable "c"	Deliverable "f"	Deliverable "cc"

The timeframe for the roadmap can vary, from a week to a month, a quarter, or even a year. You can adjust the roadmap duration according to your market and organizational needs. For enterprises, we find quarterly roadmaps effective, while small businesses benefit from monthly roadmaps, and the consumer market often benefits from biweekly updates.

For example, for our hypothetical quantum component business, the roadmap might look something like this:

Objective	Customer Key Result	Business Key Result	First Six Months	Next Six Months
Emerge as the acknowledged industry standard for quantum components and simulation software	- "At least 80% of companies using our solution adopt it at least once a month for a year."	"More than 100 companies are proactively utilizing our simulation solution by the conclusion of the first year."	Initiative 1: Simulation software	Initiative 3: Integrated buying experience
	"At least 40% of companies ordering and utilizing our chips continue placing orders every quarter."	"We have secured orders from more than 20 companies for our components by the culmination of the first year."		Initiative 2: Quantum components

By employing this structure, you create a clear visual representation of how your product development efforts are aligned with objectives and key results, enhancing communication and strategic planning.

Communication and Stakeholder Management

Think of it like planning a surprise party for a friend. It's not just your party; others care about it too. These are your *stakeholders*. A stakeholder is anyone interested in what you're doing; they could be affected by it or have something to contribute.

Now, picture a product you're developing. It's not just you working on it, right? There are team members, customers, bosses, investors, and maybe even users. They're all stakeholders because they care about the product's success in some way.

Just as you'd share party plans, you must communicate your product roadmap to stakeholders. Why? They want to know what's happening! They want to grasp where the product is going, what's happening when, and how it aligns with the goals.

Stakeholders are like teammates in a game. If everyone knows the game plan, they work better together. Sharing the roadmap means sharing the product's future plan. This keeps everyone on the same page, reduces confusion, and ensures they all work towards the same target.

Effective Communication Steps

1. *Understand their interests*: Different stakeholders care about different aspects. Focus on what matters most to each group. For instance, investors might care about the business impact, while developers could want technical specifics.

2. *Define meeting goals*: Know what you want from this communication: buy-in, approval, motivation, gap identification, or something else.

3. *Customize content*: Tailor the content based on the audience and your goals.

4. *Be clear*: Use simple language and visuals to explain the roadmap. Skip the jargon that may confuse others. The table format we discussed helps.

5. *Visual aids*: Diagrams, charts, and timelines help folks grasp the plan faster. Visuals show the bigger picture.

6. *Timing matters*: Pick a time when everyone can focus. Don't surprise them with abrupt info; plan a proper discussion.

7. *Ask for questions*: Encourage questions. It's fine if they don't get everything immediately. You're there to help.

Sometimes, stakeholders may have worries about the roadmap. Deal with them like this:

1. *Listen*: Let them express their concerns. Understand what's bothering them.

2. *Explain*: Provide more info to clear up misunderstandings. Often, concerns arise from lacking information.

3. *Problem-solving*: If real issues exist, work together to find solutions. Maybe adjusting the roadmap can address their worries.

4. *Stay open*: Keep communication open. Check if their concerns are resolved or if new ones pop up.

Remember, communication isn't just telling what's happening. It's also about hearing their thoughts and collaborating to improve things. When everyone's in sync, your product's journey becomes smoother and more successful!

Measuring and Tracking Progress

Now that you have your roadmap and you're set to put it into action, tracking progress is essential. You'll watch the timelines closely to ensure the initiative stays on schedule as per the roadmap. If any risks pop up, your risk mitigation plan should come into play. Sometimes, a new risk might arise, or your risk plan might not work as expected. Don't worry—it's a common situation!

Ensure your team and stakeholders are informed about these developments. Open, consistent communication is key here. Share the risk details, the steps you've taken, the results, and what assistance you need. Remember, you won't get help if you don't ask for it.

But the journey doesn't end when the deliverable is complete. It's time to measure the key result's progress. Put on your analyst hat and run queries to understand how customers are engaging with the product. This helps you enhance the product, making it more appealing to customers who need it for their tasks. While data analysis gives you the "what" (customer behavior), you need to talk to customers to understand the "why."

This ongoing process informs you if your roadmap (or plan to reach the objective) is working or needs adjustments. Getting this feedback swiftly with minimal effort (lean testing) is super beneficial. It saves both money and time. Money can be earned back, but time doesn't wait for anyone.

Adjusting the Roadmap as Needed

Imagine you're on a road trip with your friends. Along the way, you realize that the route you initially planned isn't working out. Maybe there's unexpected traffic or an exciting detour you want to take. What do you do? You adjust your route to make the journey smoother or more exciting. Similarly, in the world of product management, you might need to adjust your roadmap.

Let's say things aren't going as expected or you've stumbled upon a fantastic opportunity that could speed up your progress. In such cases, it's time to consider adjusting your roadmap. Here's how you can do it effectively:

1. *Re-evaluate objective and key result*: Before making any changes, review your main goal and key result. Make sure they still align with the updated information. Avoid changing them on a whim; base your decisions on data and accountability.

2. *Re-evaluate initiatives and timeline*: Next, take a look at your planned initiatives and their timeline. This is often where adjustments are needed. You might add new tasks or remove some existing ones or speed up existing ones. Remember, change is OK.

3. *Estimate cost and manage risk*: Assess the costs and potential risks of your adjustments. Having a clear understanding of these factors helps you plan and execute the changes more smoothly.

4. *Create the new roadmap*: Using the new information, funding, cost estimates, risk assessment, and dependencies, create your updated roadmap.

5. *Communicate and align*: Share the adjusted roadmap with stakeholders. It's crucial to get their alignment and support for the changes.

6. *Execute and measure*: Start working on the adjusted roadmap. Keep tracking your progress and assessing if you're on track to achieve the objective.

Remember what Jeff Bezos, Amazon's founder, says about decision-making: there are two types of decisions. Type 1 decisions are like jumping off a cliff; once made, there's no turning back. Type 2 decisions are more reversible. The key is to recognize which type of decision you're dealing with. For Type 2 decisions, don't hesitate; make and execute them quickly.

You might make some adjustments that don't pan out as expected, and that's OK. Learning from these experiences makes you wiser and more skilled. With time, you'll have the skills, knowledge, and experience to navigate even the trickiest of adjustments.

So, make as many Type 2 decisions as you can. While there's no guarantee of success, not making any decisions guarantees you won't succeed. Embrace adjustments, adapt to changes, and keep moving forward on your product journey.

Summary

In this chapter, we explored the essential elements of crafting a quantum roadmap for your development project. We started by laying the groundwork with product roadmaps and OKRs, providing you with a solid framework for planning and execution. You learned how to articulate clear objectives, pinpoint key deliverables, and make accurate resource and timeline estimates to keep your quantum project on track. We also delved into the critical task of risk assessment and mitigation, highlighting the specific challenges quantum development teams may face. To cap it off, we showed you how to structure outcomes effectively, manage stakeholders, measure and track progress, and, when necessary, make adjustments to your roadmap to thrive in the ever-evolving quantum landscape.

CHAPTER 7

Integrating Quantum Computing into an Existing System

The emergence of quantum computing represents a paradigm shift in the world of technology, promising unprecedented computational power to tackle complex problems that were once considered insurmountable. As quantum computing technologies continue to advance, organizations across various industries are eager to harness this potential. However, the transition to quantum computing is not a mere plug-and-play affair. It requires a systematic and thoughtful approach to seamlessly integrate quantum capabilities into existing systems, processes, and workflows.

In this chapter, we embark on a journey into the intricate world of quantum computing integration. We will explore the crucial steps, strategies, and considerations that organizations must navigate to unlock the transformative power of quantum computing while ensuring the cohesion and reliability of their current systems. From data preparation and software development to security and maintenance, this chapter offers a comprehensive roadmap for those venturing into the quantum frontier, enabling them to make informed decisions and leverage the quantum advantage effectively. Welcome to the realm of integrating quantum computing into existing systems, where innovation meets pragmatism.

Introduction to Integrating Quantum Computing

Picture having a powerful computer at your disposal yet encountering problems that it can't tackle swiftly. That's where quantum computing enters the scene; it's like a superhero computer capable of swiftly solving specific challenges. However, integrating this quantum superhero into your existing system will present its own challenges..

D. Agarwal et al., *Productizing Quantum Computing*, https://doi.org/10.1007/978-1-4842-9985-2_7

Within this section, we'll delve into the essentials of quantum computing integration. We'll cover the hurdles and the thrilling prospects it presents. Think of it as introducing a new friend to your group: understanding them and learning how to collaborate seamlessly.

Before we embark, it's important to evaluate whether the integration would truly benefit your customers or users who employ your solutions. Consider these key criteria:

- *Job complexity:* Is the task you're addressing highly intricate, exceeding classical computers' capabilities?

- *Use case alignment:* Does your challenge align with quantum computing's strengths, such as optimization or simulations?

- *Solution effectiveness*: Does the quantum solution demonstrably enhance accuracy, speed, or resource efficiency?

- *Classical limits:* Have classical methods reached their limits in solving your problem?

- *Quantum advantage:* Can quantum computing significantly surpass classical methods for your specific task?

- *Data complexity:* Does your data involve intricate relationships that quantum handling could excel at?

- *Feasibility:* Are practical quantum algorithms available for your challenge?

- *Technical fit:* Does quantum technology align with your existing setup and architecture?

- *Scalability:* Can the quantum solution scale alongside the growth of your system?

- *Cost and resources:* How do integration expenses compare to potential benefits?

- *Long-term impact:* Is quantum computing a viable and sustainable solution for the foreseeable future?

- *Risks and challenges:* Are you prepared to address potential complexities and uncertainties?

- *Collaboration potential:* Could collaboration with quantum experts enhance the integration process?

By weighing these criteria, you'll arrive at a well-informed decision about quantum integration. Remember, every situation is different, in some cases integrating quantum computing will be appropriate; in others, it may not be.

Much like learning to ride a bike, the initial steps might be a touch tricky. However, armed with the right guidance and a willingness to learn, you'll soon find yourself adept at seamlessly integrating quantum computing into your established systems. Let's embark on this exciting journey together!

Analyzing Existing Systems

Before you introduce something new into your environment, it's crucial to assess what's already in place. Think of it as tidying up your room before introducing new furniture. In this section, we'll delve into the process of analyzing your existing systems to ensure they're prepared for the quantum upgrade.

Much like checking if your phone has enough storage before downloading a new app, you want to ensure your current systems can handle quantum computing. You need to verify their compatibility and assess if the upgrade truly enhances the situation.

Here's how you can effectively analyze your existing systems:

1. *Identify goals:* What quantum-powered outcomes are you aiming for? Do you have specific problems you anticipate solving more efficiently or newly accessible challenges? Clearly defining your objectives guides your analysis.

2. *Understand your systems:* Take a deep dive into your present systems. What software and hardware components do you employ? How do they interact? This is akin to understanding the pieces of a complex puzzle.

3. *Compatibility check:* Ensure your systems can communicate with quantum computers. This is like confirming if your vintage radio can play modern tunes.

4. *Solution check:* Will integrating quantum computing genuinely accelerate processes or enable previously unsolvable challenges? Sometimes, the effort involved might outweigh the benefits.

5. *Data compatibility:* Evaluate if your data harmonizes well with quantum computing. Imagine incorporating a new ingredient into a cherished recipe. Will it enhance the flavor or disrupt the balance?

6. *Resource assessment:* Quantum computing might necessitate different resources. Think of it as needing a distinct kind of fuel for your vehicle. Do you possess what's needed to power quantum processes?

7. *Integration strategy:* Based on your analysis, sketch out how quantum computing will be integrated. Similar to planning where new furniture fits into a room.

8. *Readiness for change:* Occasionally, adjustments might be required to align existing systems with quantum technology. This parallels rearranging your closet to accommodate new clothing items.

9. *Scaling considerations:* Most importantly, make data-driven decisions about how quantum components or integration will scale alongside your current software. Consider factors such as user load and new use cases.

Analyzing your existing systems lays the foundation for a smooth transition. It shields you from unforeseen challenges and empowers well-informed decisions. Just like embarking on a puzzle without understanding how the pieces fit together isn't ideal, embarking on quantum integration without a clear system understanding can pose challenges.

So, get ready to delve into your systems and ascertain how quantum computing can harmoniously blend into your technological landscape. Just like assembling a puzzle, each piece needs to fit seamlessly for the grand picture to emerge beautifully.

Data Preparation for Quantum Computing

Imagine you're about to bake a cake. Before you begin mixing ingredients, you gather and prepare everything. Similarly, in the realm of quantum computing, data needs to be primed before utilizing it within a quantum computer. This section offers insights into the process of data preparation tailored for quantum computing.

Picture baking a cake with messy, disorganized ingredients. The outcome may not be favorable. Similarly, inadequate preparation of quantum data could yield inaccurate results in quantum computations. Effective data preparation is akin to tidying up your kitchen for a successful baking session; it lays the groundwork for productive quantum computations.

Much like baking necessitates specific ingredients, quantum computing requires meticulously prepared data. But, before delving into the quantum realm, just as you'd ensure ingredients are fresh, data needs to be in good shape too. Just as a tidy workspace facilitates baking, cleaning up your data enhances quantum computation accuracy.

Furthermore, quantum computers are particular. They have a preferred way of data consumption. Thus, your data must be formatted correctly for a quantum computer's comprehension. This involves encoding your data, which can be thought of as translating it into a language quantum computers understand. Quantum computers work with qubits (quantum bits), distinct from traditional bits. Therefore, you're essentially translating information into a quantum-friendly dialect.

Unlike classical bits that hold one of two possible states (0 or 1), qubits can exist in numerous states simultaneously, akin to a spinning top simultaneously up and down. The right state must be prepped for your computation, comparable to selecting appropriate tools for baking.

Quantum computers, like us in the kitchen, sometimes make mistakes. Noise and errors can disrupt calculations. Part of data preparation involves readying your data to endure these small glitches.

Quantum computers employ gates to execute operations on qubits, which is analogous to how classical computers use electronic gates. You're tasked with mapping your data onto these gates logically. This mirrors accurately adhering to a recipe's steps for a delicious outcome.

In essence, data preparation for quantum computing equips your information to seamlessly integrate with quantum processes. Just as proper ingredient prep forms the foundation of a delectable dish, preparing quantum data ensures accurate, efficient quantum computations.

Quantum Computing Software Development

Think of quantum computing like a new type of recipe. You have new ingredients and a different way of cooking. Quantum software development is about creating these new recipes for quantum computers. In this section, we'll talk about how quantum software development works.

Just like regular computers need software to run, quantum computers also need special software. But here's the twist: quantum software uses the unique abilities of quantum computers to solve problems that are too complex for regular computers.

When you cook, you follow a recipe. Quantum software is like writing a recipe for quantum computers. You tell the quantum computer what to do step-by-step using special quantum "commands."

Writing quantum software is a bit tricky. Quantum computers are sensitive and can get easily confused. It's like teaching a robot a dance; you need to be very precise. If you make a mistake, the result can be completely wrong.

In the quantum world, there are special algorithms, like magic tricks for computers. They can solve complex problems much faster than regular computers. Quantum software developers create and use these algorithms to get the best out of quantum computers.

Specific programming languages, tools, and SDKs are required for quantum computing because it's fundamentally different than classical computing. This is similar to the move from 2D graphics to 3D graphics found in XR (e.g., virtual reality, augmented reality, and mixed reality). In addition to different tools, it requires a different approach in terms of how we think about problems and how we solve them.

When you cook a new recipe, you taste it to make sure it's good. In quantum software, you use a simulation of the quantum computer to see if the program works, and once you have resolved the most obvious issues, you'd run it on actual quantum hardware. Sometimes, it might not work perfectly, and you need to adjust the recipe (in other words, the code) to make it better.

Quantum software development is like creating new magic spells for computers. It lets us solve problems that were impossible before. As quantum technology grows, better quantum software will unlock even more amazing possibilities.

Integration Strategies

Imagine you're in the kitchen with a variety of ingredients to cook a delightful meal. You can either blend them all together haphazardly or follow a recipe that cleverly combines them. Integrating quantum computing into existing systems is a bit like cooking; you need a well-thought-out strategy to make everything harmonize seamlessly. In this section, we'll delve into various strategies for integrating quantum computing.

1. *Side dish strategy:* Think of quantum computing as a "side dish." Utilize it to solve specific problems that your current systems struggle with. It's akin to adding a special sauce to your meal to enhance its flavor.

2. *Gradual integration strategy:* Adopt quantum computing step-by-step. Begin with small tasks and observe how they blend with your existing systems. This approach is like introducing one new ingredient at a time to see how it transforms the dish.

3. *Parallel processing strategy:* Delegate tasks to quantum computers while your regular systems manage others. It's similar to having two chefs collaborate to prepare different segments of a meal.

4. *Full overhaul strategy:* Picture renovating your kitchen entirely. Swap some of your current systems with ones designed to seamlessly integrate with quantum computing.

5. *Hybrid strategy:* Combine the strengths of both realms. Employ quantum computing for tasks where it excels, while relying on your regular systems for others. It's like creating a fusion dish that highlights each ingredient's unique qualities.

Selecting the appropriate strategy hinges on your objectives and your systems' adaptability to change. It's akin to choosing the perfect recipe for a specific occasion, just as you wouldn't prepare a complex dish for a quick weekday dinner.

Having a well-defined integration strategy mirrors following a recipe for triumph. It guarantees that quantum computing becomes a valuable asset to your technological landscape. Similar to skillfully blending the right ingredients to create a delectable meal, integrating quantum computing with a fitting strategy can yield robust and efficient outcomes.

Choosing the Right Quantum Computing Provider

Imagine you're in the market for a new car. With so many choices—various brands, features, and prices—you aim to find one that suits your needs, budget, and transportation plans. Selecting a quantum computing provider is quite similar—you're on the lookout for the perfect match that aligns with your goals and aspirations. In this section, we'll discuss how to make the right choice when it comes to quantum computing providers.

Here are some key factors to consider when evaluating providers:

- *Capabilities*: What tasks can their quantum computers handle? Do they possess the computational power required for your specific problems?

- *Technology*: What quantum technology does the provider utilize? Different technologies come with distinct strengths and weaknesses.

- *Ease of use*: Is their platform user-friendly? A seamless experience matters.

- *Support*: Is their customer support reliable? In case of challenges, having strong support can be invaluable.

- *Scalability*: Can their system grow alongside your needs? You don't want to outpace your chosen quantum provider if your demands increase.

- *Cost*: What's their pricing structure? It should align with your budget and investment plans.

- *R&D pace*: How much do they invest in research and development? Their past breakthroughs and the speed of delivering innovations can give you insights into their commitment.

Just like you'd select a car that suits your driving habits, opt for a provider that's in sync with your goals. If you're a business tackling intricate problems, a provider with robust capabilities might be necessary. For those in the learning and experimentation phase, a beginner-friendly provider could be a better fit.

Before fully committing, many providers offer trial periods, akin to test-driving a car before making a purchase. This trial phase lets you gauge whether the provider's technology and support align with your requirements.

Much like you'd ask friends about their car ownership experiences, seek insights from industry peers. Gather opinions on different providers to gain a well-rounded perspective that aids in your decision-making process. Just as shared anecdotes about cars can offer valuable insights, the experiences of others can guide you toward the ideal quantum computing provider for your needs.

Debugging and Error Correction in Quantum Computing

Imagine constructing a complex LEGO set. Occasionally, a piece might not fit perfectly, necessitating a search for the issue and a subsequent correction. This mirrors the process of debugging and error correction in quantum computing. This section will provide insight into identifying and rectifying mistakes in the quantum realm.

In a manner akin to spotting a missing LEGO piece, quantum computing demands the identification of where a misstep occurred. Mistakes can arise because of noise, errors, or other contributing factors. Recognizing the discrepancies between anticipated and actual outcomes is crucial.

- *Errors*: Within quantum computing, gates are employed to execute operations on qubits. Yet, these gates can inadvertently introduce errors, similar to using a slightly malfunctioning tool. The task at hand is then to rectify the tool or navigate around the issue.

- *Noise and disturbances*: The realm of quantum computations is vulnerable to the intrusion of noise and disturbances, necessitating the implementation of strategies to safeguard against these disruptions.

- *Quantum error codes*: These codes are analogous to concealed messages, aiding in the identification of missteps. Crafted as distinctive patterns, quantum error codes unveil the nature of errors and their origin, much like a trail of breadcrumbs leading to the root cause.

- *Error-correcting circuits*: These circuits function as a safety net, intercepting errors and rectifying them. Their role is to ensure the precision of quantum outcomes.

Many of these concepts have been elaborated upon in previous chapters of this book.

Addressing quantum errors bears resemblance to solving a puzzle. Intriguingly, the process of correction itself can inadvertently introduce fresh errors, necessitating a delicate equilibrium between identification and rectification, all while avoiding compounding the issue. Just as skilled puzzle-solving requires precision and a strategic approach, so too does the process of debugging and error correction in the realm of quantum computing.

Testing and Validating Quantum Computing Systems

Think of the process of testing and validating quantum computing systems like baking a cake. Before presenting the cake to your guests, you take a small bite to ensure its deliciousness. Similarly, in quantum computing, it's crucial to ensure everything functions well before putting it to use. Testing is akin to identifying any issues or errors within your quantum system, while validation confirms that the system operates correctly.

- *Quantum experiments*: In solving any large-scale problem, it's often helpful to break it into smaller problems and build proof-of-concept solutions to each. This will allow you to then build these into a cohesive design addressing the issue at large.

- *Benchmarking*: This involves comparing your quantum system's performance against established standards. These benchmarks offer insights into the efficiency, accuracy, and dependability of quantum processors and algorithms. Consider this as evaluating your cake's taste against what's universally regarded as a delectable cake. Benchmarking informs you how well your system fares compared to others.

  Here are various types of quantum benchmarks:

  - *Gate fidelity*: This gauges the precision of quantum gates, which are fundamental components of quantum operations. It quantifies how closely actual quantum gate operations match the ideal ones.

- *Quantum volume*: An IBM metric, it combines multiple aspects of quantum processor performance, such as gate fidelity, qubit connectivity, and error rates. It provides a single value reflecting the complexity of tasks a quantum computer can handle.

- *Randomized benchmarking*: This assesses the error rates of quantum gates and operations. It involves applying random gate sequences and analyzing the fidelity of resulting states against a reference state.

- *Variational quantum eigensolver (VQE) efficiency*: VQE finds the ground state energy of a quantum system. Its efficiency benchmark compares the energy estimate obtained from a quantum computer with the expected result.

- *Quantum error correction*: This evaluates the effectiveness of error correction codes in quantum systems. Benchmarks involve simulating or executing error correction procedures and measuring their efficacy.

- *Quantum supremacy tasks*: These involve executing tasks infeasible for classical computers within a reasonable time frame. Google's Sycamore experiment exemplifies a quantum supremacy benchmark.

- *Quantum communication benchmarks*: These assess the efficiency and security of quantum communication protocols, like quantum key distribution (QKD).

- *Runtime benchmarks*: These measure the time needed to execute specific quantum algorithms or operations, offering insights into quantum computer speed and efficiency.

- *Entanglement generation and measurement*: This benchmark evaluates a quantum processor's ability to create and measure entangled states, crucial for many quantum algorithms.

- *Noise and error analysis*: Benchmarks quantify noise levels and error rates in quantum processors, characterizing errors affecting quantum operations.

- *Quantum machine learning benchmarks*: These evaluate quantum algorithm performance in machine learning tasks, comparing them with classical machine learning methods.

It's vital to note that quantum benchmarks evolve as quantum technologies progress. These benchmarks serve as tools for researchers, developers, and stakeholders to gauge the advancement of quantum computing systems and algorithms, propelling improvements in the field.

- *Validation tests*: Validation is akin to receiving a nod of approval for your cake. You conduct specific tests to ensure your quantum system produces accurate results. Checking if your system solves problems correctly is pivotal. For quantum software, you might use continuous integration and continuous deployment (CI/CD) pipelines where code is tested before being promoted towards a release branch.

- *Measuring accuracy*: Similar to ensuring your cake is baked to perfection, in quantum computing you gauge how closely your outcomes align with expected results. This reveals the reliability of your quantum system.

- *Error rates*: Visualize counting how many times ingredients spill while baking. In quantum computing, error rates illustrate how often your system commits mistakes. Lower error rates indicate superior performance.

- *Real-world testing*: Just as you want your cake to please everyone's palate, your quantum system should be versatile. Real-world testing evaluates your system's performance across various tasks and challenges. Alpha and beta testing programs serve as valuable mechanisms here.

- *Scaling up*: When baking numerous cakes, a larger oven becomes necessary. Similarly, as your quantum system expands, confirming its continued accuracy is essential. Testing illuminates how well your system handles growth.

Imagine not tasting your cake before serving it; it might disappoint your guests. Similarly, without testing and validation, your quantum system might yield inaccurate results, leading to misguided decisions. Thorough testing ensures the reliability and credibility of your quantum computations, much like a delectable cake savored by all.

Maintenance and Upkeep of Quantum Computing Systems

Imagine your quantum computing system like a car. Just as a car requires regular check-ups and care for smooth operation, your quantum system demands maintenance and attention to sustain its optimal performance. Just as a well-maintained car lasts longer and performs better, consistent maintenance of your quantum system ensures its reliability and efficiency over time.

Consider taking your car for routine check-ups to detect minor issues before they escalate. Similarly, regular checks on your quantum system help detect potential glitches early and rectify them.

- *Software updates*: Just as your phone receives updates for improved functionality, your quantum system might require software updates. These updates enhance performance, address bugs, and introduce new features.

- *Hardware care*: Like a car's engine requires oil and care, your quantum hardware necessitates adequate cooling, cleaning, and protection for seamless operation.

- *Component replacement*: When a car part malfunctions, you replace it to ensure safe driving. Analogously, in quantum systems, worn-out or outdated components might need replacement to uphold performance.

- *Performance monitoring*: Similar to tracking your car's fuel efficiency, monitoring your quantum system's performance helps detect changes and promptly address any issues.

- *Contingency plans*: Cars can unexpectedly break down, so you keep a spare tire. In quantum computing, devising backup plans for unforeseen problems helps maintain operations even during glitches.

- *Security and safety*: Just as you secure your car to prevent theft, safeguarding your quantum system from threats and unauthorized access is pivotal.

- *Documentation*: Maintaining records of your car's maintenance is important. Similarly, documenting changes, updates, and fixes for your quantum system preserves its history and decisions.

Consistent car maintenance ensures safety and reliability in driving. Similarly, regular upkeep of your quantum system guarantees its dependability in accurate computations. This practice forestalls unexpected issues and prolongs the lifespan of your quantum computing setup. Although maintenance demands effort, the outcome is worthwhile: a consistently reliable tool for tackling intricate problems.

Security Considerations for Quantum Computing Integration

Imagine you have a secret treasure chest that you want to keep safe. You would lock it securely and give the key only to trusted people. Similarly, when integrating quantum computing into existing systems, security becomes crucial to protect your data and information from potential threats. Think of your data as a valuable treasure. You wouldn't want anyone to steal or tamper with it. Security ensures that your data, systems, and sensitive information are safeguarded from hackers, unauthorized access, and other risks.

- *Zero trust access*: Think about a valuable treasure you need to protect. Normally, you might build strong walls and trust only a few guards. But with "zero trust," you don't automatically trust anyone, not even the guards. Instead of relying on a big wall and a few guards, you check everyone who wants to enter, regardless of who they are. This way, only the right people can access the treasure. It's like checking everyone's ID before they get close. In quantum systems, security is vital. Zero trust means always double-checking and verifying someone's identity, even if they seem trustworthy. This prevents unauthorized access and threats. It's like ensuring only those who know the secret code can approach the quantum system. Zero trust adds an extra security layer to keep your quantum system and its important data safe. This involves using strong passwords, encryption, and other measures such as two-factor authentication.

- *Just-in-time authorization*: Imagine even in your personal house, teenagers don't have access to your bank accounts or valuables until needed. Similarly, for accessing quantum system code or data, there should be variable levels of authorization and an approval system that grants higher access only when necessary.

- *Securing communication*: When you send important messages, you want them to reach only the intended recipient. In quantum computing, securing communication ensures that the data you send and receive remains private and can't be intercepted.

- *Protecting sensitive data*: Your personal information is precious, so you keep it safe. Similarly, with quantum computing, you must protect sensitive data such as financial records or personal details by encrypting them.

- *Identifying risks*: Just like checking for weak spots in your castle's walls, identifying risks in quantum computing integration means finding vulnerabilities that hackers might exploit. This helps you strengthen your defenses.

- *Regular security checks*: Just as your home needs regular security checks, your quantum systems require continuous monitoring. Regular security assessments help you spot and fix weaknesses promptly.

- *Employee training*: You teach your family about safety measures. Similarly, in a business setting, educating your team about security practices helps everyone understand how to keep the quantum system safe.

- *Secure development practices*: When building something valuable, you use strong materials. In quantum integration, using secure coding practices ensures the software you develop doesn't have vulnerabilities that could be exploited.

- *Backup plans*: Keeping a copy of your treasure map in a safe place is like having backup plans and disaster recovery strategies in case of security breaches to minimize damage.

- *Keeping up with threats*: Just like staying updated with news, keeping up with new security threats and techniques helps you adapt your security measures accordingly.

Security acts as a robust shield protecting your valuable information and quantum systems. Just as you take measures to secure your possessions, integrating quantum computing requires careful planning and vigilance to shield your data and systems from potential dangers. It's an ongoing effort to keep your digital treasure chest secure from modern-day threats.

Summary

This chapter explored 10 crucial waypoints, each dissecting vital facets of the quantum integration process. Starting with an introduction to the quantum revolution, the chapter guided you through the evaluation of their existing systems, the intricacies of data preparation for quantum algorithms, and the essentials of quantum software development. It then explored diverse integration strategies, from selecting the right quantum computing provider to dealing with the unique challenges of debugging and error correction in quantum computing. Rigorous testing and validation processes, alongside ongoing maintenance and security considerations, were thoroughly covered. By offering practical insights, real-world examples, and expert advice, the chapter equipped you, whether seasoned IT professional or curious novice, with the knowledge and tools required to navigate the quantum frontier effectively. In doing so, it facilitated the convergence of existing systems and quantum capabilities, reshaping the landscape of computation and innovation. Welcome to the future of computing, where the fusion of quantum power and existing infrastructure paves the way for unprecedented advancements and problem-solving capabilities.

CHAPTER 8

Releasing Quantum Computing Products

In this chapter, we'll discuss the knowledge and skills necessary to successfully release quantum-based products or features to customers and end users.

If you're in the process of integrating quantum features into an existing product or enhancing an already-existing feature, feel free to skip the first three sections as the content may already be familiar to you.

However, if you're working on a brand new product, whether you're part of a large tech company, an organization, or a startup starting from scratch, the first three sections are crucial for your journey. We strongly recommend taking the time to read and understand them.

It's common for some people to view aspects such as monetization, positioning, acquisition, activation, and product releases as secondary considerations. But that perspective isn't the most effective approach. When developing a product, everything—from the core value it offers, how it's delivered, the user experience, its positioning, marketing, and more—needs to be integrated. This ensures that customers have a seamless and cohesive experience from the moment they become aware of your product to when they acquire it, activate it, engage with it, retain it (especially for cases where frequent usage isn't the norm), and eventually pay for it. The goal is to create a cycle where users not only repeatedly use your product but also share positive word-of-mouth recommendations. Your product should be designed to be so valuable and relevant that customers choose to engage with it every time they encounter the need it addresses.

© Dhairyya Agarwal, Shalini D and Srinjoy Ganguly 2023
D. Agarwal et al., *Productizing Quantum Computing*, https://doi.org/10.1007/978-1-4842-9985-2_8

How to Monetize the Product

Monetizing your product isn't just about covering costs; it's about extracting value from your customers while solving their needs. This section will guide you through the process of pricing your quantum product in a strategic way.

Often, people consider product pricing as an afterthought. It's not just about costs and margins or blindly following competitors' prices. Instead, let's dive into some economics basics.

Profit equation

Profit = Revenue – Cost. Cost consists of the fixed cost (rent, marketing) and the variable cost (manufacturing cost, customer acquisition). Revenue comes from what you charge, how many times you charge, and the number of customers.

Maximizing profit

Our goal is to maximize profit by lowering costs (fixed or variable) and increasing revenue. Our focus is on increasing revenue.

In this section, we'll focus on monetization, which involves determining what to charge and how often to charge.

1. *Setting business goals:* Define your business goal. Are you aiming for maximum revenue or quick market share growth? Understand if you want to attract early adopters or gain a larger customer base.

2. *Understanding customer segments:* Identify customer segments and the value you offer them. What are they willing to pay for? Engage in interviews and surveys to understand their pricing thoughts.

3. *Researching pricing:* Use methods like interviews, surveys, and advanced techniques such as conjoint analysis and price sensitivity analysis to gauge customers' willingness to pay.

   - *Van Westendorp price sensitivity meter:* This method involves asking customers about different price levels to determine an acceptable price range.

   - *A/B testing:* Offer various prices to different segments and analyze their reactions for optimal pricing.

4. *Defining pricing strategy:* Based on insights and your goals, decide on the following:

    a. What to charge? Create different price plans for upselling, cross-selling, or both.

    b. When to charge? Does the customer pay based on up front or after the fact?

    c. How to charge? Consider the value offered and trigger frequency for charging. Explore payment models such as subscription (monthly, quarterly), pay-as-you-go, or lifetime up-front payments.

5. *Experimenting:* Monetization is a science. It involves experiments and adjustments to find the right fit for your product and market.

By understanding the basics, researching customer segments, and experimenting with pricing strategies, you can effectively monetize your quantum product. It's not guesswork; it's a well-informed approach to extract value while satisfying your customers.

Working on Activation

Activation is like turning on a car's engine after it's been parked for a while. It marks the moment when your customers begin using your product for the first time. This phase is crucial because it's where customers start experiencing the value that your product promises to offer. Activation involves a series of steps, generally categorized as follows:

1. *Setup*: This step involves guiding customers through the actions needed to complete the initial setup, ensuring they have the ability to perform the core actions that deliver value. It's like helping them get ready to accomplish the tasks they've hired your solution for.

2. *Awareness*: Here, you lead customers to perform the core actions or tasks required to fulfill their goals. This step is about making them aware of how they can utilize your product to achieve what they need.

3. *A-ha! moment*: The "a-ha!" moment occurs when customers
    successfully perform the core actions or tasks, leading to
    satisfaction and a sense of accomplishment. This is when they
    realize the true value of your product.

However, various challenges can arise in each of these steps:

- *Lack of data*: Sometimes, you might not have enough customer data
  to deliver value effectively, especially during the initial stages.

- *Learning curve*: Customers might struggle to learn how to use your
  product efficiently, causing frustration.

- *Distractions*: Numerous distractions can divert users' attention from
  the main tasks, leading to drop-offs.

- *Monetary requests*: Introducing payment requests early can deter
  customers from proceeding further.

- *Discomfort*: Physical or mental discomfort during the process can
  discourage users from continuing.

- *Competing solutions*: If alternatives are easier to try or use, customers
  might choose those over your solution.

To address these challenges, consider employing psychological principles and
tactics.

- *Fogg's behavioral model*: Understand that behavior is a result of
  motivation, ability, and triggers. Leverage this model to guide users
  through activation steps.

- *Persuasion principles*: Employ principles such as reciprocation,
  commitment, social proof, liking, authority, and scarcity to motivate
  users to complete tasks.

- *Simplify setup*: Improve usability, reduce decision-making
  complexity, and guide users progressively using checklists.

- *Value showcase*: Clearly demonstrate the value your quantum
  product offers during onboarding to motivate users.

- *Personalized reminders*: Use reminders to nudge users who drop off
  during the setup process.

- *Focus on awareness*: Simplify the process with a "do, show, tell" approach, catering to the customer's desire for ease and speed.

- *A-ha! moment motivation*: Employ principles like social proof, authority, incentives, and triggers to encourage users to experience the a-ha moment.

In addition, continuously gather user feedback and employ analytics to track behavior and preferences. Identify popular features and areas for improvement. Based on user insights and data, continuously refine your onboarding process and engagement strategies. Iterate and optimize to enhance the overall user experience.

Remember, activation is not a one-time event but an ongoing process to ensure users experience and appreciate the value your quantum product offers.

Understanding Your Acquisition Channels

Understanding your acquisition channels is like knowing which roads lead to your party venue. These channels are the pathways through which potential customers discover and engage with your quantum product. Identifying the right channels and optimizing their effectiveness is crucial for successful acquisition as the cost of acquisition can make or break your business. Here are some key steps to consider:

- *Identifying relevant channels*: Think of different ways people can hear about your party. Similarly, identify where your target audience hangs out and how they gather information. Research online platforms, social media networks, industry forums, and other places where your potential customers are likely to be. These are the channels you'll focus on for acquisition.

- Direct sales:

  - *Sales team*: Engaging with customers directly

  - *Direct mail*: Sending physical materials to addresses

- Online channels:

  - *Website*: Central hub for information and transactions

  - *E-commerce platforms*: Online marketplaces for transactions

- *Social media*: Engaging and promoting on platforms

- *Email marketing*: Targeted emails for updates

- *Content and marketing channels*:

  - *Blogs*: Informative articles and updates

  - *Webinars*: Online seminars for education

  - *Podcasts*: Audio content on trends

  - *Video Platforms*: Visual content for demos and tutorials

- *SEO*: Optimizing content for search engines

- *Partnerships and alliances*:

  - *Channel partners*: Collaborative promotion

  - *Resellers*: Selling through distributors

- *Networking and events*:

  - *Trade shows*: Showcasing products

  - *Networking groups*: Building connections

- *Traditional media*:

  - *Print advertising*: Ads in publications

  - *TV and radio advertising*: Broadcast commercials

- *Influencer and affiliate marketing*:

  - *Influencers*: Partnering with online figures

  - *Affiliates*: Earning from referrals

- *Customer service and support*:

  - *Customer service center*: Assisting customers

  - *Online chat*: Immediate website support

- *Mobile apps and platforms*:

  - *Mobile apps*: Accessing products

- *Community and forums*:

  - *Online communities*: Discussion platforms

- *Diversifying your approach*: Imagine inviting people through social media, email, and word of mouth. In acquisition, diversify your efforts across multiple channels to maximize your reach. Don't rely solely on one platform; instead, use a mix of channels to engage a broader audience.

- *Testing and experimentation*: Think of trying different routes to your party venue. Similarly, test different acquisition channels to see which ones yield the best results. Use A/B testing, run experiments, and analyze data to understand which channels are driving the most qualified leads and conversions.

- *Monitoring and analytics*: Imagine checking a map to see which roads are busiest. In acquisition, use analytics tools to monitor the performance of each channel. Track metrics like click-through rates, conversion rates, and cost per acquisition. This helps you understand which channels are providing the highest return on investment.

- *Optimization and scaling*: Just as you might choose to take the faster route to your party, optimize the channels that are performing well. Allocate more resources to the channels that yield the best results and refine your strategies based on the data you collect.

- *Continuous learning*: Imagine learning about a shortcut that nobody else knows about. In acquisition, stay updated with industry trends and changes in consumer behavior. Continuously learn from your analytics, customer feedback, and market insights to refine your acquisition strategies.

Remember, just as parties have different guest preferences, different customer segments might respond better to different acquisition channels. By understanding and optimizing your acquisition channels, you can effectively connect with your target audience and invite them to experience the value of your quantum product.

Positioning the Product

Positioning is like finding the perfect spot for your product on a crowded shelf, making it stand out and catch the customer's eye. It's about defining how your quantum product is distinct and valuable in the market. Effective positioning helps potential customers understand why they need your product and why it's better than alternatives. It involves crafting a clear message that resonates with your target audience.

Your unique value proposition is like the special ingredient that makes your dish unique and irresistible. It's a concise statement that outlines what makes your product exceptional. Consider these steps:

1. *Identify customer needs*: Understand your target customers' pain points, challenges, and desires. How can your quantum product address these needs better than others?

    - Positioning is like tailoring your message to different guests at a party. Your quantum product might have diverse benefits for different users. Segmentation involves dividing your target audience into smaller groups based on characteristics, needs, or preferences. For each segment, develop positioning tailored to their specific requirements. This ensures that your message resonates more strongly.

2. *Highlight key benefits*: List the most significant benefits your quantum product offers in terms of customers. Is it faster calculations? More accurate results? Reduced complexity? Make these benefits clear.

3. *Address competition*: Research your competitors and identify their strengths and weaknesses in terms of customers. What sets your quantum product apart? How does it solve problems differently?

4. *Craft a compelling message*: Combine these elements into a concise and compelling statement. This statement should communicate the unique value your quantum product brings to customers.

- Positioning is about creating an emotional connection. Think of your quantum product as a solution that relieves pain points or fulfills desires. Identify the emotional impact your product can have on customers. Does it save time, reduce stress, boost confidence, or enable innovation? Incorporate these emotional triggers into your positioning.

- Positioning is like summing up your product's essence in a single sentence. A positioning statement typically follows this structure:

  "For [target audience], our [quantum product] is the [category] that delivers [benefits] because [reason why it's unique]."

  This statement guides your marketing efforts and aligns your team's understanding of the product's value.

5. *Testing and refining positioning*: This is an evolving process. Continuously gather feedback from customers and monitor the market. Are customers resonating with your positioning? Are there changes in the competitive landscape? Adapt your positioning as needed to ensure it remains relevant and effective.

Positioning your quantum product effectively is crucial for attracting and retaining customers. It's about creating a clear and compelling narrative that communicates how your product meets customers' needs in a way that competitors can't. A strong positioning strategy helps your quantum product become the go-to solution in a competitive market.

Preparing for Market Release and Launch Strategies

Preparing for market release is like setting the stage for a grand performance. It's the final countdown before your quantum product steps into the spotlight. This phase involves meticulous planning, coordination, and execution to ensure a successful launch that captures attention and drives engagement. Launching your quantum product the grand performance. It's the moment when you unveil your product to the world and make a lasting impression. A well-planned market release and launch strategy at the right time can significantly impact how your quantum product is received and adopted by your target audience.

- *Finalize product readiness*: Just as a chef taste-tests a dish before it's served, ensure your quantum product is fully functional, thoroughly tested, and aligned with customer expectations. Address any last-minute glitches, refine user interfaces, and confirm that all features are working seamlessly.

- *Create a smooth user experience*: Creating a smooth user experience is like ensuring a seamless flow in your play. Make sure your quantum product's onboarding process is user-friendly and intuitive. Deliver a frictionless experience that helps users quickly grasp the value and the functionality, essentially two different things.

- *Set launch goals and metrics*: Preparing for market release is like defining the destination before a journey. Set clear goals for your launch—what you aim to achieve, such as user retention, usage, market share capture, or broader brand recognition. Identify key metrics to measure your launch's success, such as website traffic, engagement rates, or user feedback.

- *Plan distribution channels*: Selecting distribution channels is like choosing the best roads to reach your destination. Determine where and how you'll make your quantum product available. This could be through your website, app stores, partner platforms, or specialized industry channels.

- *Leverage influencers and partnerships*: Leveraging influencers and partnerships is like having guest stars in your play. Collaborate with key industry influencers, thought leaders, or strategic partners who can help amplify your quantum product's launch message and reach a wider audience.

- *Plan your communication*: Planning your communication is like scripting the dialogue for each act of a play. Develop a comprehensive communication plan that outlines what messages will be shared, when, and through which channels. Craft compelling narratives that highlight your quantum product's unique value proposition.

- *Develop marketing materials*: Preparing for market release is like designing invitations for your event. Create compelling marketing materials that communicate your quantum product's benefits, features, and positioning. This includes website content, social media posts, videos, blog articles, and press releases.

- *Train customer support*: Training customer support is like having ushers ready to assist guests at an event. Ensure your support team is well-versed in your quantum product's features, benefits, and potential issues. This helps them provide timely and accurate assistance to customers.

- *Coordinate with stakeholders*: Coordinating with stakeholders is like ensuring all performers are in sync for a show. Collaborate with your team, partners, influencers, and supporters to ensure everyone is aligned with the launch timeline, messaging, and activities.

- *Timing is key*: Timing is like choosing the perfect moment for a play's premiere. Select a launch date that aligns with industry trends, events, or relevant milestones. Avoid launching during periods of low market activity or when your target audience might be less engaged.

- *Choose the right launch type*: Choosing the right launch type is like selecting the genre of your play. Decide on the launch approach that suits your quantum product and business model. Options include a quiet launch (soft launch), grand launch event, phased launch, or even a beta release to a select group of users.

- *Create a buzz*: Creating a buzz is like building anticipation for the upcoming performance. Use teasers, sneak peeks, and engaging content to generate excitement about your quantum product before the official launch. This piques curiosity and encourages people to learn more.

- *Conduct a dry run*: Conducting a dry run is like rehearsing a play before opening night. Simulate the launch process, from website updates to customer interactions, to identify any potential hiccups. This practice ensures everything runs smoothly on the actual launch day.

- *Secure technical infrastructure*: Securing technical infrastructure is like ensuring the stage is set and lights are working for a performance. Confirm that your website, app, or platform can handle the anticipated traffic and load. Address any security vulnerabilities to prevent data breaches.

- *Launch countdown*: The launch countdown is like the final moments before the curtain rises on a play. Double-check all elements, have your team ready, and ensure that your marketing materials are scheduled to go live at the right time.

Preparing for market release is a critical phase that sets the tone for your quantum product's success. A well-executed launch captures attention, generates excitement, and drives initial adoption. By meticulously planning and coordinating each step, you create a strong foundation for a successful market debut.

Managing Customer Expectations

Managing customer expectations is like setting the stage for a theater performance. It's about creating a clear understanding of what your quantum product offers, ensuring that customers know what to expect, and delivering on those promises. Effective expectation management is crucial for building trust, satisfaction, and long-term customer relationships.

- Transparency in communication is like providing a program booklet before a play. Clearly and honestly communicate what your quantum product can and cannot do. Avoid overhyping or making exaggerated claims that could lead to disappointment later.

- Setting a realistic value proposition is like conveying the genre and theme of a performance. Clearly define the specific problems your quantum product addresses and the benefits it offers. Help customers see how your product fits into their needs and goals.

- Providing clear feature descriptions is like listing the acts and scenes of a play. Break down your quantum product's features, functionalities, and capabilities. Use simple language to explain what each feature does and how it adds value.

- Setting realistic timelines is like informing the audience about intermissions. Clearly communicate the expected timeframes for implementing, using, and experiencing the benefits of your quantum product. Avoid promising instant results if that's not the case.

- Managing customer support expectations is like having ushers available during intermissions. Outline what type of customer support you provide, including response times and available channels. Help customers understand where and how they can get assistance.

- Sharing success stories is like displaying reviews and accolades before a performance. Highlight case studies or testimonials from satisfied customers who have experienced positive outcomes with your quantum product. This builds confidence and realistic expectations.

- Addressing limitations up front is like warning about scenes with sensitive content. Be transparent about any limitations, constraints, or known issues of your quantum product. This prevents customers from forming unrealistic expectations and feeling disappointed later.

- Providing clear guidelines is like informing the audience about theater etiquette. Educate customers on how to effectively use your quantum product, maximize its benefits, and troubleshoot common issues. This empowers them to make the most out of their experience.

- Regular updates are like evolving acts in a play. Keep your customers informed about new features, enhancements, and improvements you're working on. This demonstrates your commitment to continually enhancing their experience.

- Collecting and acting on feedback is like listening to audience reactions and reviews. Encourage customers to share their experiences and suggestions. Use their feedback to make necessary adjustments, address pain points, and improve your quantum product.

- Continuous communication is like maintaining engagement during the intermission. Stay connected with customers through emails, newsletters, social media, or user communities. Share insights, tips, and updates to keep them engaged and informed.

Managing customer expectations is an ongoing effort that ensures customers have a clear understanding of your quantum product's capabilities and benefits. By being transparent, setting realistic expectations, and delivering on your promises, you build trust and loyalty. Effective expectation management contributes to customer satisfaction, positive word-of-mouth, and a strong reputation in the quantum computing landscape.

Post-Launch Monitoring and Feedback

After the curtains rise on your quantum product's market release, the show isn't over. In fact, it's just the beginning of a new act—the phase where you closely observe, assess, and refine your performance. Post-launch monitoring and feedback are your critical tools for ensuring your quantum product continues to captivate its audience and evolve with their needs.

1. *Observing the audience response*: Just like an attentive director gauges the audience's reactions during a play, you'll need to keep a watchful eye on how your quantum product is being received. Utilize analytics and metrics to track key indicators such as website traffic, conversion rates, user engagement, and social media activity. This data provides valuable insights into your product's performance and user behavior.

2. *Listening to feedback*: Every great performer thrives on feedback, and your quantum product is no different. Encourage users to share their experiences, opinions, and suggestions. This feedback loop helps you understand what's resonating with your audience and what might need refinement. Whether through surveys, reviews, or direct interactions, actively solicit input and make your users feel heard and valued.

3. *Iterating for improvement*: Armed with data and feedback, it's time for the director's cut. Identify areas where your quantum product could be enhanced or optimized. Just as a play goes through rehearsals and refinements, your product can benefit from iterative updates. Prioritize the most impactful changes and improvements based on the insights gained from monitoring and user feedback.

4. *Staying relevant and adaptive*: In the ever-evolving landscape of quantum computing, staying relevant is key. Regularly update your product to align with the latest industry trends, user preferences, and technological advancements. Embrace the agile approach of continuous improvement to maintain your quantum product's relevance and competitive edge.

5. *Engaging and communicating*: After the curtains fall, it's not time to disappear backstage. Keep engaging with your audience through post-launch communications. Share updates, new features, and improvements to keep your users excited and informed. This ongoing engagement strengthens the relationship between your product and its users, fostering loyalty and advocacy.

Just as a successful theater production involves constant refinement and attention to the audience's reactions, the post-launch phase of your quantum product requires vigilant monitoring and responsiveness. By closely listening to feedback, adapting based on insights, and consistently improving your offering, you ensure that your quantum product remains a star performer in the quantum computing arena.

Summary

The chapter explored the fundamental aspect of monetizing these products, emphasizing the importance of defining a clear value proposition and pricing strategy. Next, it tackled the critical task of activation, guiding you on how to ensure that customers can readily use and benefit from the quantum product. Understanding acquisition channels came into focus as we discussed the various avenues through which customers can discover and access quantum offerings.

Positioning the product is another crucial aspect, emphasizing the need to communicate its unique value in the quantum landscape effectively. Preparing for market release and launch strategies provides you with insights into planning and executing a successful product launch, including marketing, outreach, and timing considerations. Managing customer expectations becomes paramount, shedding light on how to set realistic expectations and deliver on promises in the quantum computing arena.

Post-launch monitoring and feedback mechanisms are explored, highlighting the significance of continuous improvement and adapting to customer needs and preferences. This equips you as individuals and organizations venturing into quantum computing-based products with the knowledge and strategies required to navigate the complex landscape of product release. By following these guidelines, you can maximize the chances of success, effectively monetize their quantum innovations, and contribute to the ongoing evolution of the quantum computing industry.

CHAPTER 9

Challenges and Risks in Productizing Quantum Computing

Quantum computing is one of the few fields in the broad tapestry of technological evolution that inspires fascination, promise, and intricacy. Quantum technology heralds a paradigm shift, threatening to reshape the fabric of computational capabilities as it hovers at the intersection of profound physics and cutting-edge computing. However, challenges are involved in turning this quantum potential into genuine, marketable products. Understanding the complexities of quantum computing becomes a strategic and technical need for product managers navigating this new environment.

This chapter discusses the many hazards and difficulties of commercializing quantum computing. We start a thorough investigation that covers everything from early technological problems to wider societal repercussions, workforce transitions, and changing regulatory environments.

Identifying Challenges in Productizing Quantum Computing

As a rapidly developing area of technical innovation, quantum computing has the potential to revolutionize several sectors by providing computational capacity that traditional systems can only imagine. But like with any newly developed technology, there are many obstacles to overcome before actual products or solutions—such as breakthroughs in material science enabling ultra-efficient batteries, quantum

D. Agarwal et al., *Productizing Quantum Computing*, https://doi.org/10.1007/978-1-4842-9985-2_9

and AI algorithms solving complex optimization problems for logistics, or secure communication systems leveraging quantum encryption—can be produced. Product managers must comprehend these difficulties. Let's look at the main challenges.

Hardware Limitations

These are the hardware limitations:

- The qubit, the quantum equivalent of a binary bit, is at the core of a quantum computer. Qubits, on the other hand, are innately fragile, unlike stable classical bits. The *coherence time* is a brief window of time during which a qubit's quantum state can be preserved. One approach to mitigating the short coherence time is the development and utilization of logical qubits, which are implemented using multiple physical qubits to form a more stable, fault-tolerant system. This is a promising avenue for research and development, allowing for longer computations and increasing the robustness of quantum systems. For product managers, understanding the advancements in this area is vital to gauge the real potential and limitations of current quantum hardware. The data may be lost or corrupted if procedures are not carried out within this time range. This translates for product managers to establish reasonable expectations for what the present quantum gear is capable of. It also emphasizes the necessity of tight cooperation with research teams to measure advancements in coherence times.

- Because of the fragile nature of qubits, quantum operations are prone to errors. While faults can also occur in conventional systems, finding and fixing quantum errors can be significantly more challenging. Product managers must be cautious about making high-accuracy promises when the underlying hardware might not deliver on them consistently. The main focus should be applications where rough estimates are acceptable or error-correction methods can be successfully used.

Cold Environments: The Quantum Refrigerator

The usual rack-mounted servers of today are not quantum computers. They need settings that are even colder than space to function! This is done to reduce any influence from outside energy sources that can damage the qubits. While this may be interesting for those interested in science, it causes practical problems for product managers. Quantum computer deployment on-premises becomes a difficult task. Because of this, most quantum computing services may be cloud-based at first, necessitating robust data connectivity and secure data transmission protocols.

Software Challenges: Speaking the Quantum Language

Programming for quantum computing is a significant shift from traditional coding. It is crucial to develop new logic structures and algorithms. Moreover:

- Many well-known quantum algorithms, including Shor's factoring algorithm, are still theoretical or have been experimentally proven only in limited circumstances. Developing practical software tools based on these methods for use in practical applications can be difficult.

- Understanding the maturity of the software stack is essential for product managers. Layers of middleware and software development tools are required for quantum computing to connect basic quantum activities with usable applications. These layers, which are currently under development, significantly impact the final product's capabilities and deadlines.

Quantum-to-Classical Transition

The idea of a quantum computer as a co-processor for classical systems rather than a stand-alone device is expected. But it takes a lot of work to bring these two worlds together. A bottleneck can form when results from a quantum system are read and fed into a classical design. Determining which aspects of an issue can be solved more effectively traditionally than using quantum processing is critical.

Mitigating Technical Risks

To successfully navigate the quantum world, one must recognize technological obstacles and proactively create plans to reduce the dangers they provide. Translating quantum potentials into usable goods is extremely important for product managers. The following sections are a more detailed look at the tactics.

Researching and Investing in Error Correction Methods

Why it's important: Because of the fragility of qubits, quantum operations are prone to error. A minor environmental disruption can introduce errors.

Here is a strategy for a product manager:

- Give research and cooperation with groups working on quantum error correction top priority.

- Budgeting for quantum projects should include funding for research into potential strategies for addressing quantum mistakes, such as surface codes, cat codes, and the toric code.

- Keep abreast of developments in error correction, as they can significantly impact the dependability and performance of your products.

Continuous R&D on More Stable Qubits

Why it's important: Any quantum system's performance depends on qubit stability. The performance of every quantum system depends on how stable the used qubit technology is. Topological qubits, trapped ions, and superconducting qubits are three different types of qubit technology, and each has its benefits and drawbacks.

- Topological qubits are a viable way to create a scalable and dependable quantum computer because they take advantage of the topological characteristics of matter and are renowned for their fault tolerance and robustness against local mistakes.

- Individual ions are captured and controlled by electromagnetic fields in this method. This approach promises long coherence durations and great precision, but expanding the system to many qubits remains challenging because of complicated control methods.

- Superconducting qubits, which use superconducting circuits to take advantage of the quantum mechanical properties of superconducting materials, are now one of the front-runners and supported by organizations like Google and IBM. Compared to confined ions, they often have shorter coherence periods despite the progress.

To evaluate the potential and limitations of a quantum system while conceiving a product, a product manager must thoroughly understand the specifics of each qubit technology.

Here is a strategy for a product manager:

- Create or work with devoted R&D teams, constantly pushing qubit stability's limits.

- To ensure that your product is not reliant on a single technology's constraints or potential failures, consider diversifying your investments among various qubit technologies.

- Benchmark and evaluate qubit performance frequently to ensure the technology suits the product's objectives and user requirements.

Hybrid Systems: Bridging Quantum and Classical

Why it's important: Current quantum devices cannot currently complete all computational tasks. Where quantum systems might struggle, classical techniques succeed, and vice versa.

Here is a strategy for a product manager:

- Imagine devices where quantum computing complements existing technologies rather than taking over.

- Develop solutions that allow efficient communication between quantum and conventional processors to ensure continuous data flow. It's critical to be informed of the investments and developments being made in this space by well-known cloud providers to accomplish this efficiently. Here are some examples:

- *Amazon Braket*: You can create, test, and run quantum algorithms with Amazon Braket, a fully managed service from AWS. AWS is cooperating with quantum hardware suppliers such as Rigetti, D-Wave, and IonQ through its cloud architecture to provide a bridge between classical and quantum computing.

- *Microsoft Azure Quantum*: By collaborating with organizations such as IonQ, Honeywell, and QCI, Microsoft is constructing a comprehensive quantum ecosystem with the goal of providing seamless integration with classical computing resources. The company also regularly releases tools that improve communication between quantum and classical systems.

- *IBM Quantum*: IBM is a pioneer in the field of quantum computing. It offers cloud access to quantum computers and promotes collaborations to improve quantum software and developer tools, creating an environment where classical and quantum computing may coexist.

  Product managers can conceive systems that use the advantages of quantum computing and guarantee secure and streamlined data transfer across quantum and classical environments by coordinating with the strategies and resources provided by these cloud providers.

- Customers should know the solutions' hybrid character to have realistic expectations regarding quantum-accelerated computations.

Collaboration with Experts and Institutions at the Forefront of Quantum Research

Why it's important: Because quantum computing develops quickly, even a year's worth of new information can make decisions obsolete.

Here is a strategy for a product manager:

- Encourage collaborations with esteemed universities, think tanks, research centres, and major cloud services providers such as AWS, Microsoft Azure, and IBM Quantum, which are at the forefront of quantum computing breakthroughs, to foster a vibrant cooperative research and development environment.

- Participate in workshops, seminars, and conferences on quantum developments.

- Establish internships or programs for knowledge exchange with top quantum research organizations.

- Consider creating advisory boards with quantum experts who can provide direction, understanding, and validation.

Managing Business Risks

Business hazards exist in the difficult field of quantum computing, where technical complexities collide with developing market dynamics. Like any emerging technology, hype can frequently obscure real-world applications, resulting in misplaced investments and unrealistic expectations. As crucial as overcoming technological difficulties is risk management for product managers. The following sections highlight a thorough strategy to handle these issues.

Conduct Thorough Market Analysis to Identify Genuine Use Cases

Why it's important: The appeal of quantum's potential can make it simple to overlook actual commercial demands. Even the most advanced quantum product might need real use cases to find a market.

Here is a strategy for a product manager:

- Engage potential customers early on to understand better the problems that quantum can solve.

- Work with market research teams to learn about industries primed for a quantum disruption.

- Prioritize use cases based on their commercial need, scalability, long-term viability, and technological viability.

Educate Stakeholders About Quantum's Realistic Potential

Why it's important: Although quantum computing is frequently promoted as the solution to all computer problems, it has several advantages and disadvantages. Stakeholders with incomplete information may choose misguided tactics.

Here is a strategy for a product manager:

- Create and distribute instructional resources that help nontechnical stakeholders understand the mysteries of quantum computing.

- Hold workshops or training sessions to ensure that everyone is aware of the objectives, advantages, and restrictions of the product.

- Maintain transparency and adjust expectations by regularly communicating project updates, milestones, and setbacks.

Diversify Quantum Applications Across Sectors

Why it's important: Given the dynamic nature of the market and the growing state of quantum technology, relying on a single industry or application might be risky.

Here is a strategy for a product manager:

- Investigate a range of industries, including finance, healthcare, logistics, and energy, to find potential applications.

- Create pilot programs or prototypes suited for various sectors, collecting feedback and adjusting the product's value proposition.

- By serving a variety of industries, you may protect yourself against future downturns in any one of them while maintaining long-term growth and profits.

Continuously Monitor Technological Advancements to Pivot If Necessary

Why it's important: The quantum world is changing quickly. Today's cutting-edge technology may become outdated tomorrow.

Here is a strategy for a product manager:

- Create a particular team or procedure to monitor worldwide quantum breakthroughs.

- Consider how new tools, algorithms, and technologies might affect product development.

- Encourage an adaptable culture. Make sure the team is agile enough to make the necessary transitions if a pivot is required, whether in the technology being used, the markets being targeted, or the product's core functionality.

Addressing Ethical and Social Implications

With its groundbreaking capabilities, quantum computing not only presents technological and commercial hurdles but also digs into the murkier seas of societal impact and ethical dilemmas. As with any transformational technology, there are possible drawbacks and tremendous potential for benefit. Product managers are not only morally right to address these issues; doing so is essential for the sustainable and well-received integration of quantum technology into society. The following sections cover how.

Understand and Address Privacy Concerns

Why it's important: Cryptography is one of the first industries in which quantum computing poses a threat. Robust quantum algorithms may replace encryption techniques, safeguarding everything from Internet transactions to private correspondence.

Here is a strategy for a product manager:

- Consult cybersecurity professionals to determine the timing and gravity of quantum's potential dangers to currently used encryption protocols.

- Focus on creating quantum-resistant cryptographic techniques rather than just breaking codes if you're creating quantum products for the field of cryptography.

- Inform people clearly and concisely about the steps taken to protect their data in the post-quantum era.

Discuss the Potential Misuse in Sectors Like Financial Systems or Defense

Why it's important: Quantum computing's quick processing of enormous volumes of information makes it potentially dangerous to manipulate financial markets or create cutting-edge weapons.

Here is a strategy for a product manager:

- Encourage the team to build an ethical culture that strongly emphasizes using quantum technology responsibly.

- Establish norms and regulations for quantum applications in delicate industries by working with regulators and compliance organizations.

- If you create quantum devices with possible dual-use applications, have strict access controls and monitoring measures.

Encourage Open Dialogue Between Technologists, Policymakers, and the Public

Why it's important: Beyond affecting corporations or engineers, society as a whole is impacted by quantum computing. An informed public and policy framework is essential for the balanced development and application of quantum technologies.

Here is a strategy for a product manager:

- Organize forums, webinars, and open debates and invite specialists from other sectors to examine the effects of quantum technology on society.

- Sponsor studies on the moral implications of quantum computing in cooperation with academic institutions and think tanks.

- Contact policymakers proactively to ensure they get the knowledge they need to create informed rules and regulations.

Evaluating the Impact of Quantum Computing on the Workforce

Like all innovative innovations, quantum computing has the unavoidable consequence of changing the nature of the workforce. It significantly impacts employment, skill sets, and educational perspectives as it spreads from research labs into the commercial realm. Understanding this impact is essential for product managers from a societal standpoint and maintaining a long-lasting talent stream and an informed consumer base. The following sections cover how to maneuver around this shifting environment.

Developing Training Programs in Quantum Skills

Why it's important: As quantum technologies develop and find practical applications, there will soon be a need for experts in quantum programming, hardware design, and system integration.

Here is a strategy for a product manager:

- Develop internal quantum training courses for staff with the HR and training departments.

- Work with online education providers to create quantum-specific courses that are specialized to your business's requirements.

- Create workshops, hackathons, and boot camps to give the workforce a practical understanding of quantum principles.

Rethinking University Curriculum

Why it's important: Future talent is developed in academia, and the current curricula may still need to cover the quantum era fully.

Here is a strategy for a product manager:

- Engage with academic institutions and colleges to share information about market demands and keep the curriculum up-to-date.

- Provide students with hands-on experience by offering internships, fellowships, or capstone projects concentrating on quantum applications.

- To ensure a consistent flow of research and talent in line with market demands, support research initiatives or labs in academic institutions.

Bridging the Gap between Academia and Industry

Why it's important: The gap between academic research and commercial applications is frequently caused by the speed at which quantum technology develops.

Here is a strategy for a product manager:

- Organize frequent meetings for industry experts and academic scholars to exchange expertise.

- Create joint R&D projects where the academic community contributes theoretical analysis, and the industrial sector contributes real-world applications.

- Encourage staff members to submit research for publication, attend academic conferences, and continue participating in the literary world.

Encouraging Cross-Disciplinary Approaches

Why it's important: It is not only the purview of physicists and computer scientists to use quantum computing. Its applications cut across industries and necessitate knowledge of chemistry, biology, finance, and other fields.

Here is a strategy for a product manager:

- Encourage the collaboration of teams from many disciplines on quantum projects.

- Provide chances for cross-training so that experts in nonquantum fields can acquire fundamental quantum skills, and vice versa.

- Create multidisciplinary think tanks or brainstorming sessions to encourage creativity using many viewpoints.

Addressing Regulatory and Compliance Issues

In addition to being a technological frontier, quantum computing is a regulatory minefield. Similar to other cutting-edge technology, its rate of change frequently outpaces the development of thorough and knowledgeable rules. Product managers face difficulties in this fast-shifting regulatory environment, particularly when considering how quantum computing may affect societal norms, economic systems, and national security. The following are some tips for product managers on navigating this complex web.

Lobbying for Favorable Policies

Why it's important: Regulations can hinder innovation if they are not carefully crafted. Advocacy for advantageous policies ensures a supportive environment for the development and deployment of quantum technologies.

Here is a strategy for a product manager:

- Join forces with colleagues in the industry to speak with one voice in favor of reasonable quantum regulations.

- Engage with policymakers, providing information, knowledge, and skills to ensure they can make decisions.

- Ensure the industry's viewpoint is sufficiently reflected by participating in public consultations, workshops, or hearings where proposed regulations are discussed.

Collaborating with Legal Experts to Understand the Landscape

Why it's important: The interaction of quantum technology and legal frameworks is challenging for expertise.

Here is a strategy for a product manager:

- Legal professionals with expertise in emerging technologies and their regulatory implications should be retained or worked with.

- Provide frequent briefings or workshops to ensure the product and development teams are informed of the current regulatory landscape.

- Consult an attorney as early as possible in the product development to ensure compliance.

Staying Updated on Global Quantum Policies

Why it's important: The field of quantum computing is international. Businesses may find themselves operating in several different countries, each with its own set of regulatory requirements.

Here is a strategy for a product manager:

- Get information on global quantum legislation by subscribing to newsletters or global tech policy bulletins.

- Attend conferences or forums on the governance of new technologies that are held internationally.

- Establish an international compliance-focused team or position to ensure the organization's quantum activities are legal everywhere.

Designing Products Keeping Future Regulations in Mind

Why it's important: Quantum computing regulations are still developing. When things are made with forethought, they stay current and legal even as regulations change.

Here is a strategy for a product manager:

- Consider potential regulatory scenarios and their effects on the product's viability as you engage in scenario planning.

- Make flexibility in product architecture a top priority, allowing for updates or alterations in response to shifting regulatory requirements.

- Keep lines of communication open with regulatory organizations so that you can learn about potential future restrictions and change your product plans accordingly.

Implementing Effective Cybersecurity Measures

Cybersecurity has undergone a paradigm shift as a result of the development of quantum computing. While quantum computers have the potential to solve issues that conventional systems are thought incapable of handling, they also present a threat to the cryptographic framework that supports a large portion of the modern digital world. Addressing these cybersecurity issues becomes crucial as product managers plunge into the quantum world. The following sections cover how.

Researching Quantum-Resistant Cryptography

Why it's important: Many modern encryption techniques are at risk because of quantum algorithms' potential for big-number factoring, notably Shor's algorithm. Numerous encryption schemes might be compromised if and when large-scale quantum computers are available.

Here is a strategy for a product manager:

- Spend money on research and development developing post-quantum or quantum-resistant cryptographic techniques intended to last even in the presence of potent quantum computers.

- Benefit from the most recent theoretical developments by working with academic experts leading the cryptography field.

- Before using them in mainstream goods, pilot and evaluate quantum-resistant algorithms in controlled conditions.

Collaborating with Cybersecurity Experts

Why it's important: Cybersecurity and quantum computing have a complex relationship that calls for specialized knowledge.

Here is a strategy for a product manager:

- Form alliances with cybersecurity companies that concentrate on quantum risks and use their knowledge of practical applications.

- Set up frequent forums for knowledge exchange where cybersecurity specialists and quantum physicists can discuss and resolve shared issues.

- Cybersecurity considerations should be incorporated early in creating goods to guarantee that they are both quantum-capable and quantum-secure.

Educating Clients on the Potential Risks and Solutions

Why it's important: Clients may be ignorant of the possible threats that quantum computing poses to already-in-place security infrastructures.

Here is a strategy for a product manager:

- Create in-depth instructional materials explaining the landscape of quantum threats and the measures to mitigate them, such as whitepapers, webinars, or workshops.

- Transparently communicate how goods are changing in response to the quantum threat and the security safeguards put in place.

- Provide clients with consulting or advice services, advising them on a switch to quantum-resistant solutions and best practices.

Establishing Best Practices for Productizing Quantum Computing

The commercialization of quantum computing is a vast undertaking full of potential and complicated difficulties. Developing best practices is strategic and necessary to negotiate this terrain. These procedures serve as compasses, guaranteeing that the items are dependable, functional, and cutting-edge. A road map for product managers to implement these best practices is provided in the following sections.

Draft Standards and Guidelines in Collaboration with Experts

Why it's important: Using standards developed domestically could result in supervision in the fast-developing field of quantum computing. Collaborative drafting ensures thorough and knowledgeable rules.

Here is a strategy for a product manager:

- Create an advisory board of engineers, user experience specialists, quantum physicists, and other pertinent parties to generate ideas and establish standards.

- Review these requirements frequently, considering input from user testing, product testing, and industry improvements.

- To ensure consistency and adherence, create a repository of these standards accessible to all teams engaged in the product's design, development, and deployment.

Open-Source Some Tools to Allow Community Validation

Why it's important: In addition to encouraging openness, open-sourcing also draws on the pooled knowledge of the world's researchers and developers to produce reliable tools.

Here is a strategy for a product manager:

- Locate resources or parts that can be open-sourced without endangering private technology or commercial interests.

- Encourage contributions, feedback, and iterations to foster the development of a vibrant community around these tools.

- Establish a thorough procedure to evaluate and incorporate community contributions, ensuring they align with the general goals and requirements for the final product.

Continuously Update Practices as Technology Evolves

Why it's important: There are frequently fresh discoveries and developments in quantum technology. Continuous changes are crucial since static best practices can quickly become outdated.

Here is a strategy for a product manager:

- Create a particular team or committee that will be in charge of keeping track of quantum computing developments and evaluating the effects they will have on productization.

- Ensure that the product teams have a culture of ongoing learning and adaptation to make them flexible and open to change.

- Plan routine "Best Practice Review" meetings where teams can discuss, debate, and reevaluate procedures in light of fresh information or comments.

Case Studies in Productizing Quantum Computing

The path to commercializing quantum computing is paved with obstacles, victories, and illuminating lessons. A thorough examination of real-world endeavors teaches product managers crucial lessons. Let's examine a few well-known case studies.

IBM's Quantum Endeavors

These are the challenges:

- Enabling public access to quantum computing without sacrificing system integrity

- Teaching the fundamentals of quantum computing to a group mainly uses classical computing

These are the successes:

- The open-source Qiskit SDK was released and has since evolved into a crucial tool for quantum programming.

- The development of IBM Quantum Experience, a learning and experimentation-focused ecosystem for users, researchers, and educators.

These are the takeaways:

- Involvement in the community is invaluable. IBM boosted quantum learning and innovation by democratizing access and establishing a community.

- Qiskit is one example of an open-source project that can promote acceptance and standardization.

Google's Supremacy Claim

In 2019, Google declared that Sycamore, a 53-qubit quantum computer, had attained "quantum supremacy" by solving a task previously thought to be intractable by classical computers in a manageable amount of time.

These are the challenges:

- Scaling up the qubit count while keeping low error rates is technically challenging.

- There needs to be more skepticism about the importance of the claim among some scientific circles.

These are the successes:

- Achieving an important milestone that increased optimism for the future of quantum computing

- Driving the conversation about the state of quantum ready and its effects on business and encryption

These are the takeaways:

- "Milestone moments" like claims of superiority can energize the market and draw funding. However, to prevent misunderstandings, they should be expressed clearly.

- Peer-reviewed papers should support technological advances to give them credibility and allow for scholarly examination.

Rigetti Computing

The startup Rigetti provides cloud-based quantum computing services and wants to create the most potent quantum computers ever.

These are the challenges:

- Competing against tech powerhouses with much greater resources

- Converting cutting-edge research into marketable goods

These are the successes:

- Introducing Forest, a software environment enables programmers to create quantum algorithms for genuine quantum machines or realistic simulations

- Constructing a hybrid quantum-classical system that maximizes the benefits of both computing models

These are the takeaways:

- Startups may accelerate innovation by using agility and a clear objective.

- In the period leading up to the shift to a quantum-dominated age, hybrid systems, which combine classical and quantum computing, provide a helpful bridge.

Microsoft Quantum

A virtual conference called "Azure Quantum: Accelerating Scientific Discovery" was recently hosted by Microsoft. The fundamental point, as stated by Satya Nadella, was Microsoft's desire to promote chemistry and materials science research. With three important announcements—the release of Azure Quantum Elements, the launch of Copilot in Azure Quantum, and a statement about their work toward developing a quantum supercomputer—the firm achieved substantial advancements in the field of quantum computing.

These are the challenges:

- *Levels of quantum computing implementation*: The development of quantum computing has undergone several phases, much like the development of classical computing from vacuum tubes to integrated circuits. According to Microsoft, these stages are Foundational, Resilient, and Scale, each having its unique set of difficulties.

- *Moving beyond noisy intermediate scale quantum (NISQ)*: All quantum computers currently utilize noisy physical qubits. Addressing flaws present in physical qubits is challenging when switching from NISQ to a reliable qubit. For the creation of a scalable quantum supercomputer, the establishment of trustworthy logical qubits is crucial.

- *Addressing the limitations*: Microsoft addressed the limitations of the qubits used in NISQ computers in their "Engineering a Stable Qubit report." Scalability required a hardware qubit with inherent stability, necessitating a considerable physics advance.

These are the successes:

- *Azure Quantum Elements and Copilot*: By fusing high-performance computing, artificial intelligence, and quantum computing, Azure Quantum Elements is ready to change scientific research. On the other hand, Copilot has the potential to completely alter the way scientists interact with challenging ideas since it makes it simple for them to create simulations and easily view data.

- *Achievement of first milestone*: Microsoft achieved a topological phase of matter characterized by Majorana zero modes (MZMs) through persistent efforts. This stage could produce extremely stable qubits, opening the door to a scalable quantum supercomputer.

- *Broad quantum roadmap*: Microsoft has established a precise roadmap for creating a quantum supercomputer. The voyage begins with Majoranas' generation and control, continues with multiqubit systems resilient quantum systems, and ends with a quantum supercomputer.

Lessons Learned for Quantum Product Managers

Here are some lessons learned:

- *Keep an open mind*: Quantum computing is a continuously changing field. Product managers for quantum technologies should be flexible and open to new ideas.

- *Cooperation is important*: The development of Microsoft emphasizes the value of interdisciplinary collaboration. Their work included, among other things, quantum physics, materials science, and AI.

- *Education and outreach*: The significance of making quantum computing accessible and clear to professionals and a wider audience is highlighted by tools like Copilot in Azure Quantum.

- *Metric establishment*: Microsoft's launch of reliable quantum operations per second (rQOPS) highlights the necessity for pertinent metrics to gauge and compare the capabilities of quantum computing.

- *Clear roadmaps*: A clear roadmap, like the one Microsoft has, may direct stakeholder communication, product development, and research.

Lessons Learned and Future Directions

The journey of quantum computing from the theoretical physics' abstract to the dawn of real-world applications has been astounding. This transforming voyage provides a wealth of new knowledge and hints at a glistening future with opportunity.

The Transition from Theory to Practice

In the 20th century, academics like Richard Feynman wondered if quantum systems could replicate nature, which led to the emergence of quantum computing. What was previously an abstract idea is now clearly moving toward practical embodiment as we see quantum algorithms operating on actual quantum hardware.

Lesson: Product managers must be patient when working with deeply theoretical technologies. They frequently take some time to develop, but once they do, they might result in ground-breaking applications.

Amount of Evolution

Quantum computing has advanced in a variety of nonlinear ways. Although the fundamental theories have been around for a while, real advancements in hardware, error correction, and quantum software have recently become more apparent.

Lesson: Rapid advances in technology can occur in short bursts. Product managers must be ready to take advantage of these spurts and capitalize on unexpected improvements.

Lessons from Difficulties

Quantum computing has had to overcome skeptics, technological obstacles, and the enormous difficulty of turning quantum phenomena into scalable products throughout its development. However, the industry is now on the verge of a quantum revolution because of relentless research, teamwork, and a refusal to be discouraged by setbacks.

Lesson: The road to innovation is frequently paved with difficulties. Transformative breakthroughs can be sparked by accepting failures as teaching moments and encouraging a culture of resiliency.

Upcoming Directions

As we look forward to the quantum future, the following milestones are called for:

- The ultimate goal of fault-tolerant quantum computing is to find a quantum computer that can fix its mistakes. Realizing this will allow quantum to reach its full potential, enhancing its robustness and scalability.

- Data transmission and cybersecurity may be entirely changed by the possibility of building ultra-secure communication channels using quantum entanglement.

- There is a vision of ubiquitous quantum computing, which would take the form of hybrid devices that combine the best of the classical and quantum worlds, much to how classical computers evolved from closed labs to personal gadgets.

Lesson: There is still much to learn about quantum mechanics. While we recognize our accomplishments, keeping an eye on the future and preparing for future difficulties and opportunities are critical.

Summary

This chapter dug into the complex environment of productizing quantum computing, highlighting the necessity of strengthened cybersecurity in the quantum era and providing crucial lessons for product managers through industry case studies. The chapter explained the difficulties and successes that technical behemoths like IBM, Google, Rigetti, and Microsoft have encountered when navigating the field of quantum computing. It provided a clear timeline of the development of quantum theory, stressing the shift from theoretical concepts to practical applications and predicting an era of widespread quantum computing characterized by improved security and hybrid features. The chapter, which promoted a resilient and proactive mindset, called on product managers to foster a collaborative spirit and educational outreach, cultivate an ecosystem ready for the quantum revolution, navigate challenges with a growth mindset, and prepare for a future brimming with opportunities and advancements. It is an essential resource for comprehending the complexities of the quantum frontier. It encouraged product managers to lead in driving creative solutions with an active and transparent roadmap.

Index

A

A/B testing, 120, 125
Acquisition channels, 123–125
Activation, 121–123
Airbnb, 68
Algorithm IQ, 59
Amazon Braket, 140
Amplitude amplification, 30
Anion, 46
Artificial intelligence and big data, 36
Auxiliary qubit states, 12
Azure Quantum: Accelerating Scientific
        Discovery, 155
Azure Quantum Elements, 155, 156

B

Big-O notation, 25, 28
Bloch sphere, 14
Boolean logic, 10
Born rule, 15
Brainstorming sessions, 90
Bra-ket, 13
Bra notation, 13
Breadboarding, 71
Broad quantum roadmap, 156
Business goals, 120
Business hazards, 141
Business opportunities, 63, 64
Business sustainability, 72
Buzz, 129

C

California Consumer Privacy
        Act (CCPA), 79
Cation, 46
Circuit simulation software, 71
Classical computer construction
        materials, 11
Classical computers, 10, 11, 34, 38, 43,
        104, 113
Classical gates, 18
Classical physics, 1, 2, 6, 10, 11, 13
Classical post-processing, 35
Clients, threats, quantum computing, 150
Climate modeling, 36
Cloud computing market, 59
Commercialization of quantum
        computing, 151, 152
Communication, 128
Communication among qubits, 11
Communication and Stakeholder
        Management, 97, 99
Community and forums, 125
Computation, 9
Conducting a dry run, 129
Content and marketing channels, 124
Continuous integration and continuous
        deployment (CI/CD) pipelines, 114
Continuous learning, 125
Continuous R&D, 138, 139
Cooper pairs, 45
Copilot in Azure Quantum, 155

© Dhairyya Agarwal, Shalini D and Srinjoy Ganguly 2023
D. Agarwal et al., *Productizing Quantum Computing*, https://doi.org/10.1007/978-1-4842-9985-2

Printed in the United States
by Baker & Taylor Publisher Services